IEG WORLD BANK IFC MIGA
INDEPENDENT EVALUATION GROUP

Improving Municipal Management for Cities to Succeed

An IEG Special Study

http://www.worldbank.org/ieg

2009
The World Bank
Washington, D.C.

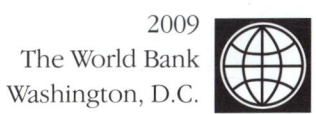

Cover: Municipal service provision is imminent in Quixadá, Northeast Brazil. Photo courtesy of Roy Gilbert.

ISBN: 978-0-8213-8043-7
e-ISBN-13: 978-0-8213-8044-4
DOI: 10.1596/978-0-8213-8043-7

Library of Congress Cataloging-in-Publication Data

Improving municipal management for cities to succeed : an IEG special study.
   p. cm.
  Includes bibliographical references.
  ISBN 978-0-8213-8043-7 (pbk.) - - ISBN 978-0-8213-8044-4 (e-book)
  1. City planning—Developing countries. 2. Municipal services—Developing countries. 3. Municipal government—Developing countries.
4. Municipal finance—Developing countries. 5. Economic assistance—Developing countries. I. World Bank. Independent Evaluation Group.
  HT169.5.I47 2009
  352.1609172'4—dc22

                              2009019206

World Bank InfoShop
E-mail: pic@worldbank.org
Telephone: 202-458-5454
Facsimile: 202-522-1500

Independent Evaluation Group
Knowledge Programs and Evaluation Capacity
Development (IEGKE)
E-mail: ieg@worldbank.org
Telephone: 202-458-4497
Facsimile: 202-522-3125

Printed on Recycled Paper

Contents

Box

Figures

Tables

Abbreviations

CDS	City Development Strategy
ERR	Economic rate of return
FINDETER	Financiera de Desarrollo Territorial SA (Local Development Fund, Colombia)
ICR	Implementation Completion Report
IEG	Independent Evaluation Group
M&E	Monitoring and evaluation
MDP	Municipal development project
O&M	Operations and maintenance
PPAR	Project Performance Assessment Report
SINIM	Sistema Nacional de Informaciones Municipales (National System for Municipal Information, Chile)
TNUDF	Tamil Nadu Urban Development Fund (India)
WDR	World Development Report

Local residents Shaoxing, China, are keen in for municipal planning to help them relocate. Photo courtesy of Roy Gilbert.

Acknowledgments

This report was prepared by the team of Roy Gilbert (task manager), Ramachandra Jammi, Kavita Mathur, and Heather Dittbrenner under the supervision of Cheryl W. Gray (Director, Independent Evaluation Group [IEG]-World Bank) and Monika Huppi (Manager, IEG Sector Evaluations). Peer review was by George Peterson (expert in municipal governance and finance, formerly of the Urban Institute) and Eleoterio Codato (former sector manager for the World Bank's Urban Anchor). The study also benefited from valuable comments and inputs by the following Bank staff: Patricia Annez, Arup Bannerji, Alain Barbu, William Dillinger, Peter Freeman, and Christine Kessides. The study team is grateful for all these valuable contributions, as well as the positive collaboration of many urban sector staff and task managers during the planning and realization of this study. The report was edited by William Hurlbut.

Director-General, Evaluation: *Vinod Thomas*
Director, Independent Evaluation Group–World Bank: *Cheryl W. Gray*
Manager, Independent Evaluation Group Sector Evaluations: *Monika Huppi*
Task Manager: *Roy Gilbert*

Low-income housing has been upgraded with water supply and sanitation in Quixeramobim, Northeast Brazil.
Photo courtesy of Roy Gilbert.

Executive Summary

Cities now host half the world's population and provide 70 percent of its gross domestic product, making them "engines of growth." Managing these economic centers well is essential for development. In nearly 3,000 municipalities worldwide, the Independent Evaluation Group (IEG) identified 190 operations as municipal development projects (MDPs). These MDPs have been the World Bank's principal instrument to help strengthen municipal management over the past decade. Evidence from this experience can provide useful input to the design of future MDPs.

The best MDPs led to stronger own-revenue flows, better financial management, improved municipal information systems, and local management of procurement. Weaker results were common in monitoring and evaluation (M&E), operations and maintenance (O&M), private finance of municipal services, and poverty focus. In these areas, MDPs can do more and do it better. MDPs serving many municipalities—called wholesale MDPs—have had better outcomes than retail MDPs, which serve just a few, although more in-depth analysis of causal factors is needed.

The purpose of this IEG special study is to illuminate the scale and scope of Bank support for municipal development and to draw specific lessons from the achievements and failures of a sample of individual projects. The findings of the study are based on a review of all 190 MDPs completed or ongoing during the period 1998–2008. In consultation with World Bank operational staff, IEG identified MDPs as projects with objectives and components focused on strengthening municipal management in cities of 12,500 inhabitants or more. Of these 190 MDPs, the 114 completed operations are the principal source for the evaluation findings. Ninety MDPs were studied through IEG desk reviews of Implementation Completion Reports, and 24 were the subject of detailed IEG field assessments, summarized in Project Performance Assessment Reports (henceforth called PPAR MDPs).

The study focuses on three dimensions of municipal management—*planning, finance,* and *service provision*—that figure repeatedly in Bank-financed MDPs. The *planning* dimension refers to the capacity of a municipality to forecast and oversee its own progress. It includes information systems, M&E, city planning, and investment strategies. The *finance* dimension refers to how a municipality manages the resources needed to provide services to its constituents. It covers financial management, own-resource mobilization, access to credit, and private funding. The *service provision* dimension refers to the capacity of a municipality to manage the services required by city residents and business people through the effective prioritization of investments, management of competitive procurement, and the ability to sustain services through O&M.

Overview of Bank Support for Municipal Management

From fiscal 1998 to 2008, the Bank committed $14.5 billion, 3.4 percent of its total lending, to these 190 MDPs. The projects have assisted nearly 3,000 urban municipalities—about 15 percent of all those in developing countries, more than a third of which are in the Latin America and the Caribbean Region. The level of MDP support to an individual municipality has varied enormously, from tailor-made technical assistance and significant investment funding to training just a few municipal staff. Up to 345 million people—IEG's estimate for the entire population of the 3,000 participating municipalities—might have benefited.

The Bank has supported MDPs in all six operational Regions. The largest number has been in Sub-Saharan Africa (27 percent of the total), and the largest lending commitment has been in East Asia and Pacific (38 percent of the total). Seventy-four percent of the 114 completed MDPs obtained satisfactory outcomes using IEG criteria, compared with 77 percent for all Bank operations. The strongest Regional MDP performers have been Latin America and the Caribbean and East Asia and Pacific, with 86 and 80 percent satisfactory outcomes, respectively.

The number of municipal clients assisted by each MDP has varied significantly. *Wholesale MDPs*—MDPs that serve seven or more municipalities—occupy the top 40 percent of this distribution. The average wholesale MDP covers 65 municipalities. Wholesale MDPs have been strong performers, with 85 percent having satisfactory outcomes. *Retail MDPs,* which serve six or fewer municipalities, make up the bottom 60 percent of the distribution. The average retail MDP serves just three municipalities. Only 67 percent of these MDPs have obtained satisfactory outcomes.

Although more analysis is needed, several factors may help explain the stronger performance of wholesale MDPs. First, wholesale MDPs can spread the downside risk of failure broadly across many municipalities. Second, competition among municipalities, a feature of all the wholesale operations reviewed, means both that municipalities that fail to meet MDP performance criteria may no longer be entitled to project support and that weak municipalities that do not qualify at the outset may become eligible for project funding later if their performance

improves. Third, the study found that wholesale MDPs allocate a significantly larger share of project spending to technical assistance and institutional development. Fourth, it is possible that municipality size is a factor—for example, if wholesale MDPs deal more with smaller, less-complex municipalities, although this could not be tested given the striking absence of population data for the municipalities they serve.

Each MDP in the portfolio of 190 has aimed to strengthen municipal management in one or more of its planning, finance, or service provision dimensions. Surprisingly, given its priority in the Bank's urban strategy and the Bank-supported Cities Alliance, better planning has been an objective of just one-third of MDPs; that is, planning has received the least attention among the three dimensions. Finance has been addressed in MDP objectives more than half the time. Service provision has featured in the objectives of nearly all of them.

Only 27 percent of the 190 MDPs in the portfolio have had project objectives focused on assisting the poor or have indicated how the poor might benefit from stronger municipal management. Earlier IEG evaluations of urban lending found twice that share. The lack of MDP poverty focus is a serious shortcoming, especially given the poverty emphasis in the Bank's urban strategy and new estimates that put the number of poor people in cities at 746 million.

In-Depth Findings from Project Assessments

In addition to the broad portfolio review summarized above, IEG undertook detailed field-based assessments of the performance of 24 MDPs. These assessments throw light on both successful practices and remaining challenges along the three dimensions of planning, finance, and service delivery.

Better municipal planning

Though planning is a priority in the Bank's urban strategy and is widely used by municipalities for mapping future city development, it was not a consistent priority in the MDPs (17 of the 24 PPAR

MDPs focus on it). Six of those 24 PPAR MDPs obtained substantial or better results in enhancing municipal information systems, one dimension of planning. A notable success was the establishment and consolidation of Chile's Web-based National System for Municipal Information. In contrast, centralized municipal information systems in Sri Lanka and Mozambique failed, in part because municipalities themselves had restricted access to them. Clearly, municipal involvement in the use of such systems is a factor of success.

M&E is another aspect of planning. When it worked well, which was rarely—only four of the PPAR MDPs had substantial results in this area—it was a hands-on instrument for the day-to-day management of project implementation and for evaluation. The weak performance of the majority of the projects often reflected inadequate attention to project results themselves. Even where MDP information systems were good—as they were in Chile, China, and Indonesia—in most cases project M&E measured only the delivery of project components and not the achievement of an operation's objectives (such as reaching the poor in the MDP in Ceará, Brazil). M&E generally worked better when countries used more widely available municipal finance data, as in Tunisia and Colombia. A very strong M&E system was built into the MDP in Kazan, Russian Federation, where some M&E performance indicators doubled as tranche release conditions, enhancing the status and importance of the M&E itself. Moreover, the Kazan municipality saw the usefulness of M&E for its own planning, and not just for fulfilling a Bank project requirement.

Relatively few MDPs attempted to strengthen city planning. Eight cases yielded substantial results, and two MDPs performed poorly. Among the successes, retail MDPs in China helped the cities of Ningbo and Tianjin develop city planning in a way that served as a model for the whole country. Sri Lanka's MDP enabled its capital Colombo to update its master plan, as Zimbabwe's did for the small city of Victoria Falls. Wholesale MDPs in Chile, Colombia, and Tunisia brought city planning to many smaller municipalities for the first time. Weaker results came in Indonesia,

where municipalities reacted coolly to the complex model of integrated planning proposed by one MDP and expressed little demand for city planning proposed in another. Notably absent was the City Development Strategy, an instrument intensely promoted by the Cities Alliance yet rarely supported in MDPs.

Municipal (nonspatial) investment strategies made headway in five PPAR MDPs. Projects in Chile, China, India, Russia, and Tunisia enabled municipalities to become more "business friendly," and two MDP clients in China rose to the top of a nationwide list of municipalities with the best investment climate in the country.

Stronger municipal finances

Most PPAR MDPs addressed the financial dimension of municipal management. This evaluation found more good results in this dimension than in the planning or service provision dimensions.

Half of these PPAR MDPs had substantial results in financial management. Good results came through project technical assistance and on-the-job learning that enabled many small municipalities in Chile, Georgia, The Gambia, India, and Tanzania to adopt computerized accounting and financial systems for the first time. Larger municipalities—such as Kazan, Maputo, and Tianjin—unified accounts and integrated financial management across their large organizations. Among the less-successful MDPs, Georgia and Uzbekistan were hindered by weak municipal capacity before the project began.

Again, half the PPAR MDPs achieved substantial results in enhancing revenue mobilization. These successful MDPs updated tax records, expanded the coverage of cadastres or land registers, and improved collections. Municipalities receiving such support in Brazil and Colombia saw their own revenues increase faster than fiscal transfers. Participating municipalities in Georgia saw significant growth of own revenues that had fallen for nonparticipants over the 2002–05 period, and own revenues of participating municipalities in The Gambia grew 50 percent faster than expected.

Weaker results for eight MDPs in Brazil, Indonesia, Mozambique, and Zimbabwe arose from political reluctance by some municipalities to raise taxes.

Improvement of municipal access to credit was an infrequent priority, with only six PPAR MDPs focusing on it at all. Of these, five had substantial efficacy in helping to "bring municipalities to market." MDPs in Colombia were particularly successful in establishing a local credit market, complete with recognized credit ratings of active municipalities; some became able to issue municipal bonds for the first time. Municipalities learned about prudent debt management through wholesale MDPs in Brazil, India, and—to a lesser degree—Georgia.

Stimulating private finance of municipal services was an objective in only five MDPs, and only one (in Colombia) yielded substantive results through private funding of water, gas, and solid waste services in several municipalities. Many municipalities lacked the expertise to staff the contract management units needed to engage the private sector. The less-successful MDPs promoted privatization of solid waste operations in Sri Lanka and Uzbekistan; these did not go far, given poor financial performance and uncertain regulatory environments. In Zimbabwe, funding of low-income municipal housing was not forthcoming from private building societies and their higher-income product lines. These weak results might have been averted with more accurate assessments of local financial markets and of the demand for municipal services that are potentially profitable.

Managing service provision

Management of municipal service provision was a priority in all 24 PPAR MDPs. In prioritizing investments in services, however, only seven MDPs successfully supported the clients' application of cost-benefit analysis with estimates of economic rates of return (ERRs). Simple yet robust estimates of ERR were made for MDPs in China, Ghana, India, Indonesia, Tanzania, and Zimbabwe. They included accurate cost figures and realistic assessments of future benefits, often measured by the higher value of urban land that has infrastructure

services. Good M&E systems helped produce some of the data needed for ERRs. In all cases, municipalities themselves were involved in the analyses. Given its successful application of ERRs in cases such as these, why did MDPs use ERR estimates so infrequently? Among the reasons given were high cost, lack of data, and externalities. But simple methods that make full use of existing data can help overcome these constraints.

Nine MDPs led to substantial strengthening of procurement management at the municipal level; other MDPs dealt with municipalities that had already handled their own procurement and needed little project support. Where municipalities handled procurement, local beneficiaries were better informed about the service improvements. Even larger municipalities, such as Kazan, Tashkent, and Tianjin, were introduced to more complex procurement packages, including international competitive bidding, by their respective MDPs.

Few MDPs had substantial results in strengthening the municipal management of O&M, which is necessary to ensure ongoing service provision. The few successful cases were in Africa, where MDPs helped computerize municipal maintenance in Tanzania and establish and fund municipal O&M accounts in The Gambia. Other successes were evident in Ghana and Tunisia. In contrast, lack of adequate O&M in MDPs led to service failures in Georgia, Indonesia, and Zimbabwe. These cases show that the risk to development outcomes can increase significantly if O&M is neglected.

Only MDPs in Brazil, The Gambia, Ghana, and Tanzania had objectives that explicitly addressed poverty alleviation or service access by the poor. Visual inspections of these projects during field missions confirmed that there were poor beneficiaries, although little data on specific poverty impacts was available. Evidence elsewhere was even thinner because of a lack of poverty focus and monitoring. The Bank still has much work to do to address its poverty reduction mission through partner municipalities. Being able to define poverty-related objectives and measure actual results of MDPs for the poor would make an important contribution.

Lessons

Several forward-looking lessons from the findings of this study are relevant for future operations and the broader municipal management agenda:

- Among the three dimensions of municipal management—planning, finance, and service provision—MDP support for strengthening municipal finance most often yielded successful results, according to field assessments. The Bank should continue to support tightened municipal financial management, own-revenue raising by municipalities, and municipalities being brought to local credit markets when appropriate conditions are present.
- Project documentation that routinely reports basic data about each client (municipality name, population, and MDP investment) is vital to developing a better understanding of the scope of MDP results.
- Wholesale MDPs that have assisted many municipalities have yielded better outcomes than retail MDPs over the past decade, but more analysis is needed to understand the precise reasons for the performance differentials. Retail MDPs might perform better if they incor-

porated more of the winning elements of wholesale MDPs, such as performance-based incentives and a focus on finance.

- More frequent use of cost-benefit or cost-effectiveness analysis would help MDPs' municipal clients select the best investments and achieve outcomes efficiently. IEG found that only half of MDPs use such tools, with the best coverage in the Sub-Saharan Africa Region.
- For M&E to succeed in MDPs, it has to be useful and not unduly burdensome to municipalities themselves, and it must keep a focus on achieving results, particularly for the poor. Strong M&E can also help reduce the expense of cost-benefit analysis by providing some of the data needed to estimate ERRs. Few MDPs have succeeded with this.
- Private financing of municipal services can be encouraged through better analysis of local financial markets and deeper understanding of demand to help municipalities gain the trust of private investors.
- Thus far, little evidence exists that stronger municipal management has benefited the poor. MDPs need to give much more attention to poverty reduction in defining MDP objectives, showing how the poor would benefit from municipal investments and how services would improve through stronger municipal management.

A moderate-income housing development in a municipality on the periphery of Mexico City. Photo courtesy of Roy Gilbert.

Management Comments

Management welcomes the Independent Evaluation Group's (IEG) study on Bank experience in improving municipal management. The World Bank recently did its own review of experience with urban infrastructure funds that serve smaller cities and towns, and one important finding was the need to understand better what works in building capacity at the municipal level.

More than 90 percent of world population growth in the next decades will be in developing country cities, many of them secondary cities and towns, whose systems are currently ill-prepared to provide services to all of their population. Strengthening management capacity is a thus a necessary condition for making cities livable. Improved and sustainable access to services is a key pillar for poverty reduction on the urban agenda.

The main lessons from the study are useful for the Urban Sector going forward: the successful role of municipal development projects' support for strengthening municipal finance; continued support for tightening of municipal financial management, raising of municipal own revenues, and bringing of municipalities to local credit markets when appropriate; the importance of project documentation for measuring results; the relative success of wholesale versus retail approaches; the need for use of cost-benefit or cost-effectiveness analysis to select the best investments and achieve outcomes efficiently; a need to strengthen monitoring and evaluation systems; analysis of local financial markets and demand to encourage private finance; and the potential role that municipal development projects (MDPs) can play in reaching the poor.

The study finding that less than one-third of the projects reviewed cited poverty alleviation as a formal objective of the project is significant and deserves further attention to understand this better. In particular, it would be useful to explore the extent to which the poverty focus in these projects may not be currently reflected in the formal development objectives of municipal development projects.[1]

Poverty reduction is at the core of the Bank's urban work and its forthcoming urban strategy. The Bank directly addresses poverty reduction in cities through a variety of instruments that are designed to address immediate and basic needs of the poor while supporting institutional and management capacity to improve and lay a solid foundation for the sustainability of services. These include slum upgrading, or development policy loans targeting policy reforms to improve access to affordable housing. Typically low-income settlements are informal and thus beyond the reach of formal service delivery. The MDPs studied in this report focus on systemwide improvements in planning, finance, and service delivery and are thus a complementary tool to ensure sustainability and access to services for all, including the poor, over the longer term.

It is important to place the role of municipal development projects in context. MDPs represent only about 35 percent of Urban Development projects prepared by the Urban Sector Board over the same time period. Among the other sector boards covered in the study, the sample includes only 2 percent of the Environmental Sector Board projects, 7 percent of Water Sector Board projects, 3 percent of Transport Sector projects, and 1 percent of Public Governance projects.

It is also important to note that there may be a reporting issue in capturing the poverty focus of municipal development projects. The determination of poverty focus in the study was based only on the project development objectives of the projects reviewed, not on the actual project content or field review. Projects focusing on systemwide improvements in accounting, planning, and tax collections are those least likely to set specific poverty objectives as the project development objective, because as explained above, impacts are more indirect and long term. Improvements in management municipal systems will help the poor over the longer term as the formal system expands its reach, but these impacts may extend beyond the period under evaluation.

Management looks forward to guidance from IEG regarding best practice on how clearer articulation of the poverty alleviation objectives and activities in municipal development projects can be captured, and on how to monitor the indirect and long-term impacts on poverty, including in smaller cities and towns, which may have limited capacity.

A review of the Bank's recent work indicates that projects with components specifically targeting the urban poor are trending upward and accounted for more than 40 percent of Urban Sector Board lending in fiscal 2008. A number of recent pieces of economic and sector work have also been developed or approved in the Urban Sector, with a strong focus on urban poverty that will help to build the pipeline. That being said, management's aim is to increase this further, reversing, for example, the decline in lending for slum upgrading over the previous two decades.

The release of the IEG report coincides with the launch of consultations on the new World Bank Urban Strategy. This is an opportune time to build on the insights from the report as we engage with clients, development partners, and civil society organizations, particularly in light of the report's call to scale up urban services to the poor. This is an agenda that calls for strengthening our analytical base, mainstreaming urban issues in Country Assistance Strategies and policy dialogue, and expanding the Bank's approaches for reaching the urban poor. Scaling up programs for delivery of services to the urban poor, innovative projects, and responsive instruments will all play a role as the Bank seeks to respond in a rapidly urbanizing world.

Chairperson's Summary: Committee on Development Effectiveness (CODE)

On March 16, 2009, the Informal Subcommittee of the Committee on Development Effectiveness considered the Independent Evaluation Group (IEG) special study *Improving Municipal Management for Cities to Succeed.* The study covered a review of the entire portfolio of 190 municipal development programs (MDPs) completed or ongoing during the 10-year period 1998–2008.

Overall Conclusions

The Committee welcomed the opportunity to discuss the IEG study, taking note that almost half of the global population lives in cities. The discussion revolved around the main IEG findings related to the poverty focus of MDPs and the three dimensions of municipal management: planning, finance, and service provision. Members remarked that the study may contribute to the overall update of the World Bank's urban sector strategy, for which the Committee was expected to consider the concept note in April. In this context, a member remarked that the report could have clarified the implications of the study findings for the Bank's urban sector strategy update. Speakers also urged management to consider a significant finding of the report, that the lack of MDP poverty focus is a serious shortcoming, especially given the poverty emphasis in the Bank's urban strategy. Management noted that the IEG study raised important questions that require further consideration, such as addressing urban poverty, taking into account the complexity of tracking this, and the reasons for wholesale MDPs yielding better outcomes than retail MDPs.

Main Issues Raised

Poverty focus

The Committee noted management's clarifications that not all MDPs may be suitable tools for addressing the needs of the poor (for example, municipal finance) and that other Bank urban projects are designed to focus on the urban poor, such as slum-upgrading projects and development policy loans that focus on policies to make housing more affordable and to target subsidies more effectively. Mention was made of the Cities Alliance global program, supported by the Bank, which has slum upgrading as a major focus. Members acknowledged the challenges of tracking urban poverty, given the shifting population and the need to consider national and municipal level linkages in addressing poverty. Nevertheless, speakers echoed IEG in urging more attention to poverty in MDP objectives, taking into consideration the distinct nature of urban poverty. A member emphasized the need to expand economic opportunities for the poor, observing that improving services for the poor is not sufficient to address urban poverty. There was a question about the decrease in poverty focus of MDPs over the years noted in the IEG study and a comment on the possible application of a Poverty and Social Impact Assessment to measure the distributional impact for Bank operations beyond policy reform programs.

Municipal services

Interest was expressed in a broader review of causality between improvements in municipal planning and finance and enhanced service delivery. As well, more information was sought on the extent to which Bank support led to increased quality and access to services, including for the poor. Some members drew attention to the importance of strengthening the operations and maintenance focus in MDPs. Though appreciating the importance of cost-benefit and economic rates of return analyses, a member cautioned about giving emphasis to such analyses in crisis situations. IEG, however, stressed the importance of economic rates of return, which can still be estimated at the latter part of project implementation.

Municipal finance

Strong financial management at the municipal level was considered one of the prerequisites to enhanced service provision, but not an end in itself. In response to a member's comment, management provided assurances that although MDPs' efforts have been successful in municipal finance, the Bank will respond to country demand and not focus solely on this dimension. Some members noted the need to consider the complex interrelations with national policies (including decentralization) and their impact on municipal fiscal management, including revenue mobilization and expenditures, as well as political factors. A member remarked that management of foreign exchange and rollover risks should be addressed as part of Bank support for municipal access to credit.

Regarding private finance, there was general agreement on the need for a good regulatory stance by municipalities that recognizes stability, effective demand, and potential for profitability. Yet a member also observed the need for more analysis of measures to increase tariffs for promoting private finance. Interest was expressed in the role of financial intermediaries and public-private partnerships at the municipal level. In addition, some members commented on innovative financing, such as the possibility of subsovereign lending without a sovereign guarantee and the use of performance-based grants. Management said that it will be holding a technical briefing on subnational lending the week of March 23, 2009.

Municipal planning

Emphasis was put on ensuring that Bank support is aligned with local city planning, including city development strategies (promoted by Cities Alliance). Some members touched on the importance of strengthening municipal institutions' capacity, and in this regard a member observed that the IEG study could have provided additional analysis on accountability and governance aspects. IEG responded that it is planning to evaluate the implementation of the Governance and Anticorruption Strategy in a few years; that evaluation can incorporate some issues encountered in the urban sector. As noted by IEG, a member underlined the need to strengthen monitoring and evaluation.

Dissemination

The engagement of Regions in the IEG special study and the strong learning element of the process were welcomed. There was a question about the presentation of the findings in other forums in the future. IEG said that after the Committee's consideration of its study, the findings would be disseminated.

Giovanni Majnoni, Chairman

Chapter 1

Evaluation Highlights

- Good municipal management of cities—which are important engines of growth—is essential to development.
- Improved municipal management has become increasingly challenging as cities grow, costs increase, and service expectations rise.
- This study reviews World Bank efforts to help strengthen three dimensions of municipal management: planning, finance, and service provision.
- This meta-evaluation assembles the findings of existing IEG assessments of municipal development projects during the period 1998–2008.

Planning city growth and conserving historic assets side by side in Ningbo, China. Photo courtesy of Roy Gilbert.

Managing Engines of Growth

Cities now host more than half the world's 6.6 billion people and produce $42.4 trillion of gross domestic product—70 percent of the world's total. Hence, the management of these important development centers is crucial.

Well-managed cities are "engines of growth," offering people opportunities to build productive lives, an idea articulated by the 1999/2000 World Development Report (WDR) *Entering the 21st Century* (World Bank 2000b, pp. 125–138). This idea was endorsed by the World Bank at the June 2008 World Cities Summit in Singapore as well as through work done for the Commission on Growth and Development[1] (Duranton 2008). It falls to local city government administrations, called *municipalities* in this report, to provide good management.[2]

Worldwide, some 31,000 municipalities—each with more than 12,500 inhabitants[3]—accommodate the world's urban population. Twenty thousand of these are in developing countries, the client base for the World Bank.[4] Each municipality typically manages a single city, and this is the unitary model of municipal management considered in this evaluation.[5]

This report reviews performance findings for three dimensions of municipal management—*planning, finance,* and *service provision*—and devotes a separate chapter to each. These dimensions accommodate the most common objectives of Bank operations to support munici-

pal management strengthening. Effective city planning can minimize spatial externalities, and rational investment planning can help allocate limited resources efficiently to local strategic priorities (chapter 3).

Proper financial management can help ensure that cities have adequate revenues and that they spend them well (chapter 4). Good preparation and delivery of urban infrastructure and services by municipalities can enhance livability for residents and productivity for businesses (chapter 5). Most Bank assistance that has sought to strengthen municipal management has been deployed within this framework.

Other dimensions of municipal management may be important in other contexts, but they are addressed by less than 5 percent of the projects covered by this study and thus have not been reviewed. They include, for example, the political dimension of strengthening local democracy, citizen participation and representation, the security dimension of policing cities, the welfare dimension of a municipality's role in providing a social safety net, and the external relations of municipalities in joining associations and forming twinning arrangements that encourage the bilateral exchange of experiences between pairs of cities. Some of these dimensions are beyond the mandate of the Bank. Other dimensions, such as the environment and climate change, housing, health, education, and culture in which municipal management is active, have been covered by other evaluations by the Independent Evaluation Group (IEG).

Evaluation of Good Municipal Management

As part of what the Bank calls *capacity building*, assessing the effectiveness of Bank assistance to strengthen municipal management requires looking for evidence that explicit municipal management objectives were achieved or that managerial improvements contributed to meeting other project objectives further down the results chain. Within the municipal management framework, this evaluation highlights notably successful operations worthy of emulation and others where shortcomings point to important lessons for improvements. The study reviewed evidence available on projects that supported the planning, finance, and service provision dimensions of municipal management.

Within the planning dimension, this evidence included information about the city, its local markets, and the local government itself, all as inputs into planning. Also, evidence of a substantial monitoring and evaluation (M&E) system would indicate a municipality ready for planning and able to manage and oversee its own progress. In addition, evidence of new and updated city plans and investment strategies would reflect a municipality able to diagnose and manage future development expectations.

In reviewing the municipal finance dimension, the study focused on examples of financial management and reporting at the local level, looking for evidence of how effectively and transparently a municipality is able to manage its resources. Thus, evidence of strong own-revenue flows would be an important indication of municipal autonomy in service delivery. Access to credit and private finance would also point to municipalities being able to provide more services.

For the dimension of managing service provision, the study searched for evidence of municipal management performance in three areas related to better access and quality of municipal services. First, it examined techniques of choosing the best performing investments for service delivery ex ante, as well as evaluating performance ex post—using cost-benefit analysis, for instance. Second, it used municipal ability to handle procurement for service provision itself as one indicator of capable municipal management. Third, it assumed that local attention to and funding for operations and maintenance (O&M) indicated municipal management that was able to sustain service provision and ensure that services remain accessible after the project assets are in place. All three areas, it should be emphasized, are concerned with the *management* of service provision, not actual service delivery itself.

Improving municipal management across these dimensions has become increasingly challenging for four reasons: ever-larger cities to administer, continuous rapid urban growth, rising costs of urban investment, and citizens' increasing expectations of the level and quality of municipal services. Large municipalities, such as the 325 in the developing world that serve more than 1 million people each, require complex organizations. In this class, the large municipality of Montevideo, Uruguay (population 1.3 million), is staffed by 8,500 people, who administer an annual budget of $261 million—which is equal in complexity to a large corporation in many countries.

Rapid urban population growth, particularly in Asia and Africa, requires that municipal management respond to demands for services and infrastructure that far exceed the capacity of existing resources and systems. Rising costs of service provision, driven by higher land prices in particular, can outstrip even what the most agile municipal financial management can provide. As expectations of municipal services rise, municipal management has to respond. Should it fail, residents and businesses might move to more successful and better-served cities. For these reasons alone, good municipal management is essential, and Bank support to strengthen it is important.

World Bank Policy Underpinning Support to Municipalities

Municipal development has long been mainstreamed in development thinking at the World Bank. Every WDR since 1990, for instance, refers to municipalities. Most recently, the 2009 WDR *Reshaping Economic Geography* sees municipalities as key players in managing city expansion as countries urbanize (World Bank 2008). A decade ago, the 1999/2000 WDR *Entering the 21st Century* stressed that municipalities have to raise substantial revenues to help provide the urban services and infrastructure that cities need to succeed as engines of growth (World Bank 2000b, chaps. 5–7).

The 2001 WDR *Attacking Poverty* posited an important municipal role in urban land tenure reform in favor of ownership by the poor (World Bank 2001, p. 94). The 2002 WDR *Building Institutions for Markets* saw municipalities playing an increasingly important role in contracting out and regulating private sector provision of services (World Bank 2002, p. 160). The 2004 WDR *Making Services Work for Poor People* placed municipalities within a "policymakers-providers-poor people" triad as potentially efficient (local) service providers to the poor when incentives are right and institutional responsibilities clear (World Bank 2004, pp. 49, 185).

Municipal management and the planning, finance, and service provision dimensions reviewed in this study remain at the center of the Bank's current urban strategy, *Cities in Transition: World Bank Urban and Local Government Strategy* (World Bank 2000a). The strategy sees municipalities as key providers of local services for improving *livability* for the poor in cities, the first pillar of the strategy.

The second pillar, *good governance,* is to be achieved through Bank support for capacity building at the municipal level, especially municipal development itself, and city planning. The third pillar, *bankability,* calls for the Bank to help municipalities achieve sound finances and credit-worthiness through better municipal financial management.

The fourth pillar, *competitiveness,* highlights City Development Strategies (CDSs) as a tool to help urban markets work better. Thus, in relation to this study, the strategy's *livability* speaks to this study's service provision dimension, *good governance* and *competitiveness* to the planning dimension, and *bankability* to the municipal finance dimension.

Findings of Earlier IEG Assessments

IEG's review of the implementation of this strategy through the Bank's urban portfolio, in its report *Improving the Lives of the Poor through Investment in Cities* (IEG 2004), found that urban projects did help improve livability but recommended more explicit and operational targets to link municipal capacity building to poverty reduction. Furthermore, that review urged more systematic M&E of the results obtained (IEG 2004, p. 31). An earlier IEG study of Bank support for municipalities, *Developing Towns and Cities: Lessons from Brazil and the Philippines* (IEG 1999), found that these operations had helped municipal reform in these two countries. A lesson of the study was that reform should be broadened beyond focusing on just one municipal instrument, such as property tax, to enhance own revenues.

Municipalities were a focus of IEG's Global Program Review of the Cities Alliance—part of its evaluation of global programs that are partnered by the Bank (IEG 2008). Tightly focused on upgrading low-income settlements in cities and CDSs, Cities Alliance is a multidonor partnership that aims to improve the quality of development cooperation and urban lending and strengthen the impact of grant-funded programs. This Global Program Review found that the program was well focused on its two main activities but needed to do more to strengthen M&E and the dissemination of its work. Of particular interest to the present study (as well as to the Bank's Urban Strategy) is the Cities Alliance championing of CDSs, defined as action plans for equitable growth in cities and surrounding regions.

This Study

This study is a meta-evaluation of the findings of IEG project assessments. Analogous to a literature review, the study assembles evaluation findings of what worked and what did not so that project task managers and others can find examples of good municipal management practice to emulate and replicate. They can also see shortcomings that need to be avoided or overcome. It does not determine if municipal management in general improved following Bank interventions.

The study constituted a portfolio of 190 operations,[6] called *municipal development projects* (MDPs) in this report, either completed or ongoing during the period 1998–2008. The primary focus of these operations is on urban municipalities with populations of 12,500 or more, so it does not include projects aimed at rural development. Appendix H, on methodology, details how the study identified MDPs through their "municipal" Bank activity codes and then verified with Bank Regional staff that project objectives and components really focused on strengthening municipal management.

This portfolio review laid the groundwork for the evaluation by analyzing the scope of the MDP assistance provided and the design and implementation approaches of the 190 component projects. Of these, 114 completed MDPs were the principal source for the evaluation findings. Ninety MDPs were studied through IEG desk reviews of Implementation Completion Reports, and 24 were the subject of detailed IEG field assessments, summarized in Project Performance Assessment Reports (PPARs).

The findings from these 24 PPAR MDPs, as they are called in this report, were assembled and analyzed to obtain a more in-depth view of the performance of MDP assistance. Although these PPAR MDPs do not cover every single aspect of the Bank's broad work with municipalities, and although they were not randomly selected from the portfolio, they do share the main characteristics of the portfolio as a whole, notably project size, implementation period, and distribution.[7]

In one important respect, however, they are different: 83 percent of the 24 PPAR MDPs had satisfactory outcomes, whereas across the whole portfolio only 74 percent rated satisfactory. In this report, the results of the review of the portfolio of 190 MDPs are presented in chapter 2 and the Regional appendixes (B–G); findings drawn from the 24 PPAR MDPs make up most of the material in chapters 3–5. The 76 ongoing MDPs are included in this report not to assess outcomes and results that have yet to be reported ex post, but to carry forward the review of MDP designs and approaches.

Chapter 2

Evaluation Highlights

- The Bank committed $14.5 billion to 190 MDPs in 76 countries over the period 1998–2008.
- Bank-financed MDPs have assisted 3,000 municipalities, 15 percent of the total in the developing world.
- Wholesale MDPs, each serving many municipalities, have been stronger performers than retail MDPs, which serve just a few.
- Across the three dimensions of municipal management, MDPs focus most on service provision and least on planning.
- Few MDPs focus on assisting the poor.

MDP-funded municipal water treatment plant in Pereira, Colombia. Photo courtesy of Roy Gilbert.

Bank Support for Better Municipal Management

Bank Assistance to 3,000 Municipalities

Since 1998, the Bank has committed $14.5 billion, 3.4 percent of its total funding, to 190 completed and ongoing MDPs in 76 countries worldwide. The numbers of new MDPs approved and new Bank commitments show a growth trend in the second half of the period after an uneven but generally weaker first half (figure 2.1).

The portfolio of MDPs has assisted nearly 3,000 municipalities,[1] about 15 percent of the 20,000[2] urban municipalities in the developing world. Across municipalities, the intensity of MDP support may vary considerably. It can range from tailor-made technical assistance and significant investment funding at the high end, to training just a few municipal staff, often remotely, to no physical investment at the low end. Taken as a whole, however, this support has the potential to help many people benefit from improved municipal management.

Figure 2.1: MDP Trends, 1998–2008

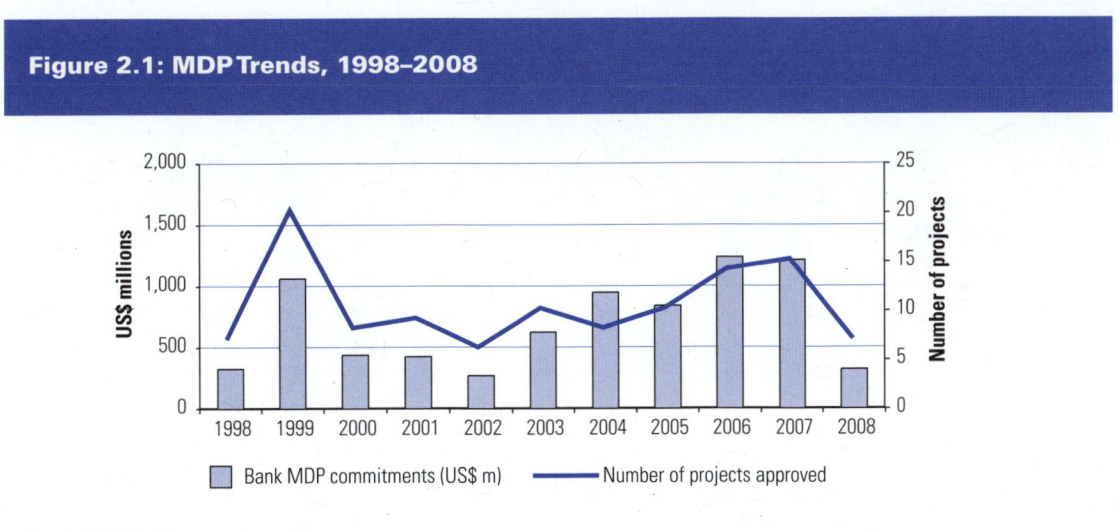

Source: World Bank data.
Note: MDP = municipal development project.

Exactly how many, however, is rarely computed accurately in Bank project documentation at appraisal, during implementation, or at completion. Of course, an accurate picture would emerge if MDPs routinely reported the number of municipalities they served and provided summary details of each one, including the name, population, and investment received. Assuming the population size distribution of the nearly 3,000 MDP beneficiary municipalities was similar to that of all urban municipalities, an estimated 345 million people would live in municipalities assisted by Bank-financed MDPs. Although not all inhabitants would be expected to benefit directly from the operations, a parameter such as this one nevertheless points to a potentially significant and extensive impact of municipal management improvements wrought by Bank-financed MDPs.

MDPs have been implemented in all Regions, with the greatest number in Sub-Saharan Africa and the largest share of commitments in East Asia and Pacific (figure 2.2). East Asia and South Asia have larger-than-average MDPs; Sub-Saharan Africa, the Middle East and North Africa, and Europe and Central Asia have smaller ones. The average Bank commitment per project is nearly three times larger in East Asia than in Africa (table 2.1). The size of individual MDPs varies considerably, ranging from $300 million-plus megaprojects in large countries—China, India, Mexico, and Turkey—to small $5 million-or-less operations with smaller clients such as Honduras, Kosovo, and Peru (details in appendix A). Also, apart from operations in Latin America and the Caribbean, ongoing MDPs have larger Bank commitments than completed ones, pointing to increasing Bank support for these projects.

MDP Approaches—Wholesale and Retail

The design of most MDPs is quite simple. The majority has just two basic components: (i) institutional development/policy reform through technical assistance and training for municipalities (and their higher-level government minders) and (ii) infrastructure and service provision through funding physical investments. Physical investments accounted for more than 85 percent of the total project costs of most of the 24 PPAR MDPs (with **Chile I** and **Mozambique I** as exceptions).

Figure 2.2: MDPs across the Regions, 1998–2008

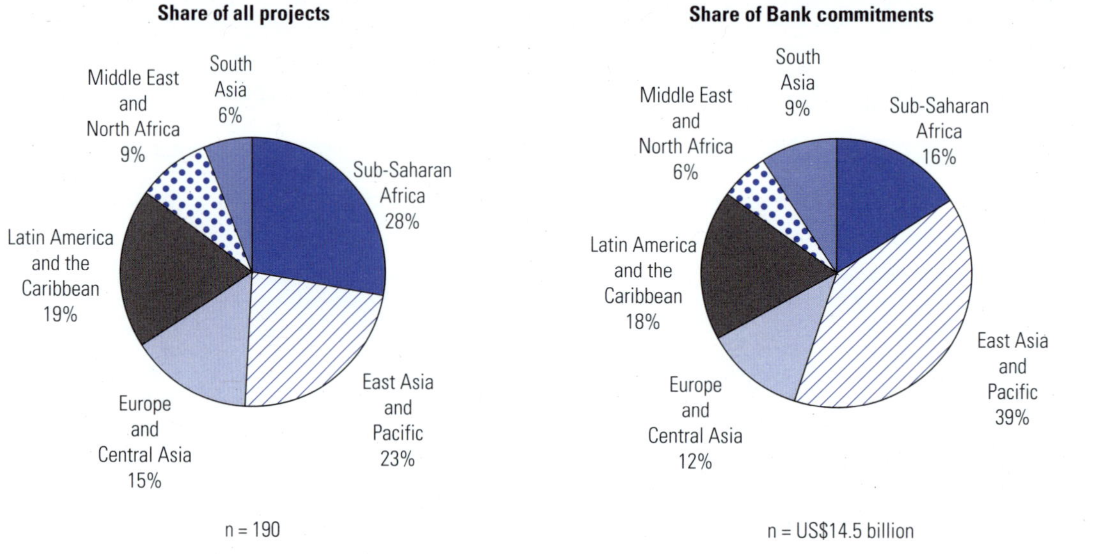

Share of all projects

Middle East and North Africa 9%
South Asia 6%
Sub-Saharan Africa 28%
Latin America and the Caribbean 19%
Europe and Central Asia 15%
East Asia and Pacific 23%

n = 190

Share of Bank commitments

South Asia 9%
Middle East and North Africa 6%
Sub-Saharan Africa 16%
Latin America and the Caribbean 18%
Europe and Central Asia 12%
East Asia and Pacific 39%

n = US$14.5 billion

Source: IEG special study.
Note: MDP = municipal development project.

Table 2.1: Completed and Ongoing MDPs by Region, 1998–2008

MDPs	Sub-Saharan Africa	East Asia and Pacific	Europe and Central Asia	Latin America and the Caribbean	Middle East and North Africa	South Asia	All MDPs
All (number)	52	44	28	36	18	12	190
Completed (number)	32	30	16	21	8	7	114
Ongoing (number)	20	14	12	15	10	5	76
MDP client municipalities[a]							
Completed + ongoing (number)	601	445	292	1,098	379	146	2,961
Average per project (number)	12	10	10	31	21	12	16
Average Bank commitment per project							
All (US$ millions)	47	129	61	74	53	112	79
Completed (US$ millions)	42	126	37	86	49	88	76
Ongoing (US$ millions)	56	136	94	53	56	146	82

Source: IEG special study.

Note: MDP = municipal development project.

a. Includes all municipalities served by at least one MDP.

Physical investments are popular with municipalities that wish to improve service provision in their jurisdictions, something that can affect the outcome of local elections. Consequently, most PPAR MDPs offered to finance such investments, but only in those municipalities that were committed to reform and institutional development. To support such reform directly, MDPs themselves funded technical assistance and training for municipalities, which accounted for up to 15 percent of the total costs of these operations. Beyond technical assistance, better management of service provision through physical investments in infrastructure also helped strengthen municipal management.

Although most MDPs embody this basic design, the number of municipal clients assisted by an individual MDP varies widely, ranging from just 1 to 257. Across all closed projects reviewed, 60 percent served 6 or fewer municipalities. These are referred to as *retail MDPs* in this study. Those serving seven or more municipalities are called *wholesale MDPs* (table 2.2).

Table 2.2: Completed MDPs with More Municipal Clients Perform Better

Quintile	Number of municipalities per project		Approach	Number of projects	Percent with satisfactory outcomes
	Range	Mean			
1	1–1	1	Retail	23	69
2	2–3	2	Retail	23	61
3	4–6	5	Retail	22	69
4	7–31	15	Wholesale	23	83
5	33–257	96	Wholesale	23	87
Overall	1–257	24	All MDPs	114	74

Source: IEG database.

Note: MDP = municipal development project.

> ### Box 2.1: Defining Features of Different MDP Approaches
>
> **Wholesale (>6 municipalities)**
> - Many municipal clients—average of 65 per project in this study's MDP portfolio—competing to participate
> - Bank wholesales project to special MDP agency that agrees on policy with the Bank and retails project services and funding to municipalities; little direct Bank contact with municipalities
> - Rules of engagement generally the same for all municipalities
> - Participating municipalities and investment subprojects not known up front
>
> **Retail (1–6 municipalities)**
> - Few municipal clients—average of three per project in this study's MDP portfolio
> - Project agreements made directly with municipalities; direct Bank contact with municipalities
> - Rules of engagement crafted for each municipality and may vary within a project
> - Participating municipalities and investment subprojects usually part of project design
>
> *Source:* IEG.

The defining features of wholesale and retail MDP designs are summarized in box 2.1. The most significant features of wholesale MDPs, found in all those reviewed by PPARs, are competition among municipalities and the use of a special MDP agency as an intermediary between the Bank and individual municipalities. Such an agency provides (that is, retails) project support to many municipal clients in the form of funding for municipal subprojects. This leaves the Bank able to concentrate its support directly on the special agency itself.[3]

Retail MDPs, in contrast, do not need such an agency. Existing government departments and the Bank itself are able to interact directly with and provide tailor-made assistance to each of the few municipalities involved. MDPs used the wholesale approach most intensively in Latin America and the Caribbean. That Region has a long history of municipal administration, where wholesale MDPs outnumber retail MDPs. For similar reasons, wholesale MDPs were also common in the Middle East and North Africa Region. East Asia hosted the largest number of retail MDPs, using this model to assist large cities in China, which are managed by unitary mega-municipalities.[4]

MDP Performance

Overall, 74 percent of the 114 completed MDPs in this study's portfolio achieved satisfactory outcomes, slightly below the Bank-wide average of 77 percent for completed projects over the same period. During the first half of the period, MDP performance was weaker, with only 65 percent of projects achieving satisfactory outcomes. Performance improved in the second half, when 85 percent were rated satisfactory. Against the 74 percent satisfactory rate for the MDP portfolio as a whole, 85 percent of completed wholesale MDPs achieved satisfactory outcomes, compared with 67 percent for retail MDPs (table 2.3). This difference between the average performance of wholesale and retail MDPs is statistically significant.[5]

Though more analysis is needed, several factors might help explain the stronger performance of wholesale MDPs. First, wholesale MDPs can spread the downside risk of failure broadly. Second, competition among municipalities in wholesale MDPs means that municipalities that fail to meet wholesale MDP performance criteria, for instance, may no longer be entitled to participate in the project. Conversely, initially ineligible municipalities that have a subsequently stronger performance can be brought on board. This gives wholesale MDPs the flexibility to allow changes in their client profile during implementation, thereby stimulating competition among municipalities.

Retail MDPs can choose their few municipal clients carefully, too, but this can only be done at the outset, and the selection criteria are not always transparent. Once chosen, retail MDP clients

Table 2.3: Completed MDPs: Performance by Region, 1998–2008

MDPs	Sub-Saharan Africa	East Asia and Pacific	Europe and Central Asia	Latin America and the Caribbean	Middle East and North Africa	South Asia	Total
Completed wholesale MDPs (7–257 municipalities each)							
Number of projects	11	8	6	13	5	3	46
Percent satisfactory	92	75	67	92	80	67	85
Number of municipalities	416	210	54	858	59	112	1,709
Completed retail MDPs (1–6 municipalities each)							
Number of projects	21	22	10	8	3	4	68
Percent satisfactory	68	82	60	75	33	25	67
Number of municipalities	22	46	15	9	3	3	98
All completed MDPs							
Number of projects	32	30	16	21	8	7	114
Percent satisfactory	75	80	63	86	63	43	74
Number of municipalities	438	256	69	867	62	115	1,807

Source: IEG special study.

Note: MDP = municipal development project.

remain the same during implementation. Policy impact leading to improved municipal management is likely to be more widespread for wholesale operations, given the larger number of municipalities affected. In addition, at 10 percent of project costs, wholesale MDPs spent more on technical assistance and institutional development than retail MDPs did; they spent only 6.4 percent.[6]

Other possible explanations for stronger performance by wholesale MDPs that might have been expected were not supported by evidence. Thus, location factors, such as wholesale MDPs being located in stronger performing Regions, did not come into play, as both types of MDP are widely represented across all Regions (table 2.3). The level of Bank financing was also not a factor, being similar for both wholesale and retail operations. An initial review did not point to substantive differences between the objectives of wholesale and retail MDPs. However, the complexity of the issues addressed by each type of MDP could affect performance and deserves further inquiry.

Another hypothesis is that wholesale MDPs perform better because they typically work with less-complicated, smaller municipalities. However, this can only be tested when MDPs routinely produce population data of the municipalities assisted, something that is missing from most of the project documentation reviewed for this study. Because the study did not examine all the possible factors, there is still a need for more analysis to elicit the precise reasons for the performance differential observed.

MDP Objectives—The Aims of Bank Assistance

All 190 MDPs reviewed here aim to strengthen municipal management in one or more of the three dimensions of this study's evaluation framework. Because project objective formulations do not always use the same language as this framework does, this study used synonym keyword searches of the formal objective statements of each MDP. This was done across all 190 operations to identify which dimensions of urban management were targeted for strengthening (details in appendix H). The results are summarized in table 2.4.

MDPs gave the most attention to service provision and the least to planning. Some MDP objectives embraced broader goals, such as improving the urban environment or assisting with decentralization, issues reviewed by other recent IEG evaluations and not dealt with in detail here.

Municipal planning, as a dimension of management, received the least attention among the aims of Bank-financed MDPs in the portfolio. Only one-third of these MDPs included better planning as an objective. This poor showing is surprising in the context of Bank support for public sector capacity building in general and Bank endorsement of CDSs in particular. As noted earlier, promoting good CDSs among cities worldwide is one of the two aims and lines of business of the Cities Alliance program, which the Bank strongly supports. Good city planning allows for city (population and economic) growth and helps provide space for environmental and other public goods, as well as locations for services and amenities that market mechanisms by themselves cannot. For the Bank itself, a greater focus on planning would have made the MDP portfolio more relevant to the goals of stronger local governance espoused by the Bank's 2000 urban strategy.

Despite the limited coverage, there have been important examples of MDPs improving planning. These are discussed in chapter 3.

Municipal finance improvement was more prominent, addressed by the objectives of half the portfolio's MDPs. Among the Regions, this received most attention in Sub-Saharan Africa and South Asia. A substantially larger share of wholesale projects—63 percent—included finance objectives than retail MDPs did—46 percent (table 2.4). Examples of actual MDP results in strengthening municipal finances are presented in chapter 4.

Nearly all MDPs have explicit goals of strengthening the ability of municipalities to better manage the provision of good-quality and accessible services. Among Regions, MDPs gave most attention to this in South Asia, East Asia and Pacific, and Sub-Saharan Africa. Wholesale and retail MDPs were equally attentive to the goal of strengthening the management of municipal services (table 2.4). Service provision's lead comes from the Bank's traditional support for the delivery of urban infrastructure. MDP experience illustrates several ways of strengthening municipal management of service provision. MDP results with respect to municipal management of service provision are illustrated through detailed references to cases described in chapter 5.

MDP Components—Instruments for Better Municipal Management

All MDPs in the portfolio chose project components to strengthen municipal management in at least one of the planning, finance, or service provision dimensions of this study's evaluation framework. Table 2.5 summarizes their distribution.

Planning, although the dimension least addressed by MDP components, is covered by components of more than half of the operations

Table 2.4: Focus of Objectives of Completed and Ongoing MDPs, 1998–2008

MDPs	Sub-Saharan Africa	East Asia and Pacific	Europe and Central Asia	Latin America and the Caribbean	Middle East and North Africa	South Asia	Total	Wholesale	Retail
Total (number)	52	44	28	36	18	12	190	72	118
Percent of all MDPs with OBJECTIVES focused on—									
Municipal planning	23	50	29	39	22	17	33	31	34
Municipal finance	62	48	54	50	33	58	52	63	46
Service provision	92	93	86	78	83	100	88	86	90

Sources: IEG and World Bank databases.

Note: MDP = municipal development project.

Table 2.5: Focus of Components of Completed and Ongoing MDPs, 1998–2008

MDPs	Sub-Saharan Africa	East Asia and Pacific	Europe and Central Asia	Latin America and the Caribbean	Middle East and North Africa	South Asia	Total	Wholesale	Retail
Total (number)	52	44	28	36	18	12	190	72	118
Percent of all MDPs with COMPONENTS focused on—									
Municipal planning	48	48	61	50	33	25	47	38	53
Municipal finance	71	43	82	44	61	50	59	59	59
Service provision	99	95	86	92	89	100	94	92	95

Sources: IEG and World Bank databases.
Note: MDP = municipal development project.

in the Europe and Central Asia and Latin America and the Caribbean Regions (table 2.5). The kinds of instruments considered here include performance-based municipal development agreements, training for municipal employees, city master plan updates, land mapping and land information systems, and preparation of strategic development programs for future investments. This report reviews MDP results from using such components in chapter 3.

Finance components are found in slightly more than half of MDPs overall, but in higher shares in the Europe and Central Asia and Sub-Saharan Africa Regions, where municipal finances have been particularly weak (table 2.5). For one-quarter of all MDPs, these components include the establishment of urban development funds to specifically finance municipal infrastructure and services, the subject of a recent Bank review (Annez, Huet, and Peterson 2008). Examples of other finance components include municipal financial rehabilitation plans, improved cash flow management, credit to fund municipal investment needs, training in budgeting and revenue generation, and technical assistance for municipalities to raise revenues from domestic capital markets. Their efficacy in contributing to good project results is reviewed in chapter 4.

Service provision components are present in nearly all MDPs (table 2.5). This predominance makes sense. After all, the ultimate purpose of strengthening municipal management is to make municipalities more effective and efficient providers of good-quality urban infrastructure and accessible services. It is through better management of services such as these that municipalities, as local public sector entities, can directly benefit users in cities.

Examples of such components in MDPs include computerized management information systems, model contracts for private sector operators, and on-the-job learning. In many MDPs this last item comes from implementing physical investments in roads; drainage; lighting; water supply (treatment plants and distribution networks); sanitation; solid waste collection and disposal; social, educational, health, and cultural facilities; urban transport (including mass transit); housing and communal services; neighborhood upgrading; and environmental rehabilitation. These are discussed in chapter 5.

Limited Attention to Poverty Reduction

Relatively few MDPs—27 percent of the total portfolio—have objectives focused on assisting the poor,[7] such as aiming to improve their living conditions through service provision to low-income areas. MDPs that omit poverty references in their objectives typically aim to improve service delivery, too, but without specifying the poor among the beneficiaries.

The sparse MDP attention to the poor is surprising in view of the urban strategy focus on poverty and the Bank's own top priority of reducing it. Municipalities have an important role in helping low-income beneficiaries, the starting point of the 2004 WDR *Making Services work for Poor People* (World Bank 2004, pp. i, 75). The absolute number of urban poor, recently estimated at some 756 million worldwide (Ravallion, Chen, and Sangraula 2007), is expected to remain high, particularly if the faster urbanization of the poor than of the population as a whole persists (World Bank 2004). Clearly, MDPs need to strengthen their poverty focus to ensure that they benefit the poor more effectively.

Chapter 3

Evaluation Highlights

- Only half the 190 MDPs in the portfolio focused on planning; the share was higher among the 24 MDPs reviewed by PPARs, where 7 projects obtained good planning results.
- Field work showed that developing municipal information systems for planning has had mixed results, with success coming from more municipal involvement.
- M&E results of evaluated projects commonly counted the delivery of project components rather than monitoring the achievement of outcomes.
- MDP coverage of city planning was thin, pointing to the need for more work in this area.

"One-stop shop" for community participation in city planning and service provision in Novgorod, Russia. Photo courtesy of Roy Gilbert.

Better Municipal Planning

Planning is a priority in the Bank's Urban Strategy and a tool widely used by municipalities for mapping future city development. For instance, planning applies to strategic spatial plans and land use. It is surprising, therefore, that only half of the 190 MDPs in the portfolio focus on city planning of any kind (tables 2.4 and 2.5).

Among the 24 MDPs reviewed by IEG's PPARs, attention to the planning dimension of municipal management was somewhat higher, with 17 projects focused on planning through their objectives or components (table 3.1). This chapter assesses the effectiveness of MDP support within each of four broad categories of planning: information management, M&E, city planning, and investment strategies. The chapter highlights successful projects, as well as examples of performance shortcomings, to inform MDP practitioners of what has worked well and what has not.

More Information for Planning

Good information about a municipality and the economic, social, and financial challenges and potential of its city are indispensable to sound planning. Good information feeds directly into M&E, enabling municipal authorities to know more about the problems they confront and progress made in solving them. Altogether, 14 PPAR MDPs specifically attempted to improve information systems. Of these, six obtained substantial or better results and eight were less successful. The remainder of the PPAR MDPs did not try to strengthen these systems (table 3.1).[1]

Perhaps the most significant MDP information success has been in Chile, where the central government's National Information System on Municipalities (SINIM, http://www.sinim.cl/) was launched (**Chile I**) and consolidated by system improvements (**Chile II**). Both operations were wholesale MDPs involving a strong higher-level agency, the Regional Development Sub-Secretariat. At this writing, SINIM holds annual data for the 2000–07 period on local finances, administration, education, and health services, as well as social and geographical indicators—250 variables altogether for every one of Chile's 345 municipalities. Being Web based and in the public domain, SINIM allows policy makers and citizens to know what their own—or any other—municipality has been doing and how well. Municipalities themselves upload the data into the database. Sustainability has been good.

The information system, created more than eight years ago, is still going strong without further Bank assistance. Although SINIM data are available to anybody with access to the Internet, municipal information systems in other countries have often been less accessible. For example, centralized information systems introduced by the **Sri Lanka MDP** in Colombo (population 2.3 million) and **Mozambique II** in Maputo (population 1.2 million) and Nampula (population 380,000) remained largely beyond the control of or even access by municipalities themselves and thus fell out of use. The clients of

Table 3.1: Summary of MDP Results in Municipal Planning

Country	MDP	Project name	Overall outcome of project	Information	M&E	City planning	Investment strategies
Sub-Saharan Africa							
Gambia, The		Pov. Alleviation & Capacity Building	M Sat	—	—	—	—
Ghana	I	Second Urban	Sat	—	—	—	—
Mozambique	**I**	**Local Govt. Reform**	**Unsat**	*	—	—	—
Tanzania	I	Urban Sector Rehabilitation	Sat	—	—	—	—
Zimbabwe		**Urban Sector & Regional Dev.**	**M Sat**	*	*	√	—
East Asia and Pacific							
China	**III**	**Tianjin Urban Development**	**Sat**	√	√	√	—
China	**IV**	**Zhejiang Multicities Dev.**	**Sat**	√	*	√	√
China	**VII**	**Shanghai Environment**	**Sat**	√	*	—	—
Indonesia	**II**	**East Java/Bali Urban Dev.**	**M Sat**	*	*	*	—
Indonesia	**VI**	**Second East Java Urban Dev.**	**M Unsat**	*	*	—	—
Indonesia	**IX**	**Municipal Innovations**	**Sat**	√	*	*	—
Europe and Central Asia							
Georgia	I	Mun. Infrastructure Rehab.	M Unsat	—	—	—	—
Georgia	II	Mun. Dev. & Decentralization	M Sat	—	—	—	—
Georgia	**III**	**Second Mun. Dev. & Decentral.**	**Sat**	*	—	—	—
Russian Federation	**IV**	**Kazan Municipal Dev.**	**H Sat**	√	√	√	√
Uzbekistan		**Tashkent Solid Waste Mgt.**	**Sat**	—	*	—	—
Latin America and the Caribbean							
Brazil	**II**	**Ceará Urban Dev/Water Res.**	**M Sat**	*	*	—	—
Chile	**II**	**Second Municipal Dev.**	**M Sat**	√	*	√	√
Colombia	**I**	**Municipal Dev.**	**Sat**	—	√	√	—
Colombia	IV	Urban Infras. Services Dev.	Sat	—	—	—	—
Middle East and North Africa							
Tunisia	**I**	**Municipal Sector Investment**	**Sat**	*	√	√	√
South Asia							
India	I	Tamil Nadu Urban Dev.	M Sat	—	—	—	—
India	**II**	**Tamil Nadu Second Urban Dev.**	**Sat**	*	*	—	√
Sri Lanka		**Colombo Env Improvement**	**Unsat**	*	*	√	—

Sources: IEG PPARs.

Note: Bold = MDPs focused on planning; √ = substantial or higher achievement of element; * = element tackled but with modest or lower achievement; — = element not attempted. (Roman numerals are attached to MDPs in their sequence in the portfolio of 190 operations, being dispensed with altogether when there is only one MDP in a particular country.) M&E = monitoring and evaluation; MDP = municipal development project. **Ratings:** H Sat = highly satisfactory; Sat = satisfactory; M Sat = moderately satisfactory; M Unsat = moderately unsatisfactory; Unsat = unsatisfactory.

the technical suppliers of such systems were central governments, meaning that the suppliers themselves rarely responded to demands from municipalities. These shortcomings clearly point to the need to involve municipalities actively up front.

A few MDPs also developed information systems at the level of individual municipalities. Through a technical assistance contract under **Indonesia IX,** a project that focused on municipal innovation, the municipality of Bogor (population 769,000) developed a lively and informative Web site to interact with and inform the public; basically, this was an online version of the municipality's earlier and successful public information booths. IEG found it still functioning well five years after completion.

In another innovation under the same project, the municipality of Surabaya (population 2.4 million) set up a hotline for citizens' inquiries or complaints about municipal services. Unfortunately, it had fallen out of use for lack of funding to maintain it. In contrast, international consulting contracts under **China III** helped the megacity of Tianjin develop a computerized traffic information system. Set up more than 10 years ago, the system is still operating without further assistance from the Bank.

Staying engaged for the long haul can help develop municipal information systems even in the most challenging circumstances. Thus, elements of a basic municipal finance information system are finally coming together after three successive MDPs in **Georgia** over 14 years. One-off efforts to improve information, as the Bank tried through **Zimbabwe's MDP,** had thin results even before the country's current crisis.

M&E

When it worked well in MDPs, which was rarely,[2] M&E was a hands-on instrument for the day-to-day management of project implementation and for conducting evaluations. Of the 24 PPAR MDPs reviewed, only 4 obtained substantial results with M&E (table 3.1). The performance of the remainder was weak, often reflecting inadequate attention to project results. Before it helps map the direction and paths a project should take, M&E begins as a planning tool; that is the reason it is considered in this chapter. For M&E to succeed, municipalities have to regard it as a useful tool for themselves, not just an instrument for government control or academic research by others. This suggests that there should be more interaction between municipalities, governments, and the Bank at the design phase of M&E.

A common weakness of M&E design for MDPs was excessive focus on monitoring the delivery of a project's components instead of measuring the actual achievement of intended outcomes. Even an MDP that otherwise excelled in information management—M&E in **Chile II**—measured only the number of technical assistance assignments completed and their cost, but not indicators of municipal governance improvements or greater efficiency in service provision, which was what the project intended.

M&E for **Indonesia II** and **VI** also ventured little beyond counting the number of subproject contracts awarded and the amount of disbursement, so M&E in those projects was able to provide the exact number of community toilets built and their precise unit costs, for instance, but not how much they were used, which proved to be very little. During field visits, IEG saw communal toilet blocks designed for 15 families being used only by 1 or 2. Though **China IV** in the Zhejiang province excelled in many other respects, its M&E did little more than count and cost the delivery of individual subprojects.

Another shortcoming often found in the M&E of MDPs was the lack of baseline data and the absence of explicit, preferably quantified targets. **Brazil II,** for instance, did not describe the living conditions of the poor at the outset in municipalities in the state of Ceará that were targeted for project improvements. Endline conditions may be easy for an evaluator to observe at completion, but how much progress they represent from the starting point can only be understood if there are also baseline data to show clearly how far the endline is from it.

Even when a baseline is known, it must be expressed in terms and units that make measurements of changes over time meaningful. High inflation, for instance, can cloud the interpretation of financial and economic indicators expressed in current values, as they were in the M&E of **Uzbekistan's MDP.** Sometimes, even good quality and quantified indicators, such as those measuring water quality of the environmentally stressed Huangpo River in Shanghai under **China VII,** are of limited use when baseline values are not comparable. In this case, baseline and endline water samples were drawn from different parts of the river. Water quality measurements that were taken from the polluted Beira Lake in the city of Colombo under **Sri Lanka's MDP** can reveal its condition today, but not the reduction of pollution—because there are no baseline data.

Experience shows that an initially weak M&E design can be enhanced during project implementation and later used effectively. This happened under **China III,** when the strong local planning team in Tianjin municipality, at its own initiative, incorporated outcome indicators to measure municipal management effectiveness that had been overlooked by the initial M&E design. **Georgia I** incorporated theoretically sound indicators in its M&E design, such as the number of days lost through schools and health centers having to close for bad weather, but there were no unit-level data available for them in the country at the time. M&E under **Georgia II** and **III** progressed to incorporate municipal finance indicators, for which data became available after more than 10 years of consistent effort.

M&E of MDPs was strongest where its focus included municipal finances. This was the case with **Colombia I** and **Tunisia I,** both of which built up extensive knowledge about municipal management in their countries. **Russia IV,** a retail operation, also incorporated a strong M&E system, albeit for one city, Kazan. But its design included clear and easy-to-measure indicators that addressed all project objectives. These included a declining municipal budget deficit, increasing targeted cash social assistance to eligible beneficiaries, and greater provision of housing and local infrastructure services by the private sector. This M&E was easy to implement and use, as the municipality of Kazan itself wanted to know these results and had the capability to collect and analyze all the necessary data.

This may not be the case in weaker municipalities. In Kazan, however, it is still in full use, two years after project completion. Part of the M&E success in Kazan comes from the programmatic structural

adjustment loan design[3] of the operation, which required the MDP to meet specific outcome targets—some as tranche release conditions—over a period of just three years.

Kazan was willing and even enthusiastic about adopting M&E because the municipality found that the information generated was useful for its own financial management purposes, not just for meeting the formal requirements of the project. During PPAR missions to review other MDPs, however, IEG heard several municipal officials say that M&E information was being collected, often at significant expense to their municipalities, just to please the World Bank. It is therefore important for project designers to ensure that the M&E will be useful for the municipalities themselves and that it still fulfills the requirements of due diligence and project evaluation. This can best be done by ensuring municipal involvement in M&E design from the outset.

City Planning and City Development Strategies

Although city planning has long been a traditional function of municipal administrations worldwide, IEG found relatively few MDPs focused on it. Of the 24 MDPs reviewed by PPARs, only 10 included a focus on city planning; most of these achieved substantial results. The remaining MDPs achieved little in strengthening such planning, not because they tried and failed, but because city planning was not on their agenda (table 3.1).

Among the successes, **China IV** in Zhejiang Province helped the municipality of Ningbo (population 720,000) update its city master plan; that plan enhanced long-term land use planning and firmly embedded the conservation of historic and cultural assets into its city center planning. **China III** also strengthened city planning in Tianjin (population 11.2 million). Several official delegations of foreign planners have visited the megacity to learn more about its successful approach to planning, especially in upgrading transport corridors and providing for solid waste and sewage disposal. As retail MDPs, these experiences point to how this approach can bring substantial improvements in planning to a few cities.

Chile II provided support for 25 municipalities to prepare local city plans. MDPs also helped municipalities update existing master plans, as they did in Tianjin, China, and Colombo, Sri Lanka, or prepare one for the first time, as in the small town of Victoria Falls (population 36,000) through the **Zimbabwe MDP. Indonesia II** supported Integrated Urban Infrastructure Development Planning, which the Bank and other donors hoped to establish as a modernized form of urban planning. But the approach was not adopted successfully by smaller municipalities in particular; they preferred to continue with the traditional sectoral approach they knew. With its municipal demand-driven design, **Indonesia IX** also had little impact on strengthening city planning, given the small demand for it among the project's municipal clients.

Although CDSs are supported by the Bank and other donors worldwide and are one important business line for the Bank-supported Cities Alliance,[4] IEG assessments found that MDPs gave CDSs very little attention. To strengthen city planning more, programming CDS work could be better coordinated with MDPs, and CDSs themselves could be integrated into MDP operations. CDSs tend to be quite diverse, and it would be helpful if the Cities Alliance could advise the Bank, MDP agencies, and municipalities which model of CDS would be best suited to a particular MDP. The current absence of CDSs would appear to call for greater synergy on this front. In addition to their strengths as forward-looking management tools, CDSs and city planning of all kinds do help municipalities know the baselines of the spatial configuration of urban development better.

Investment Planning and Strategies

Municipalities need to determine priorities for their investments, given the scarce resources available; this can be called investment planning or strategizing. Most MDPs of the 24 reviewed by PPARs have not systematically tried to do this. There were five projects that did so, and they achieved substantial results.

India II in Tamil Nadu, for example, provided technical assistance to and facilitated exchanges among 45 municipalities to help each one prepare corporate plans. These plans set out their investment priorities for 10 years. Under **Chile II,** some smaller municipalities established Local Development Directorates to coordinate municipal investment planning across sectors. Exchanges of experiences among municipalities in the Indian and Chilean cases probably mean that the dissemination of MDP experience is much wider than is obvious from the direct project results themselves.

The experience of **China IV** in Zhejiang Province helped make municipalities more business friendly. The cities of Hangzho (population 1.9 million), Ningbo, and Shaoxing (population 421,000), with planning and service provision directly assisted by the project, were among those with the best investment climate in the country, according to a 2005 survey of 14,000 firms in 120 cities throughout China (World Bank 2006).

Chapter 4

Evaluation Highlights

- Across the three dimensions of municipal management strengthening, MDP efforts in finance yielded successful results most often.
- Some small municipalities benefited by adopting computerized accounting systems for the first time.
- Some large municipalities consolidated and unified their accounts.
- Half of MDPs obtained substantial results in mobilizing municipal revenues.
- Field work showed that the results of private funding of municipal services were thin and efforts inadequately prepared.

Oversight of municipal finances in Fortaleza, Northeast Brazil. Photo courtesy of Roy Gilbert.

Stronger Municipal Finances

The majority of MDPs addressed the financial dimension of municipal management through their objectives, their components, or both (tables 2.4 and 2.5). Among the 24 PPAR MDPs, there was a strong focus on finance. Altogether, 20 of the MDPs had objectives and components related to municipal finance (table 4.1). This study compiled PPAR findings of the performance of these projects within each of four categories: financial management, mobilizing revenues, access to credit, and private finance.

Better Financial Management— Accounts and Audits

Financial management was the most frequently supported aspect among the projects reviewed, being addressed by 15 PPAR MDPs. Of these, the evaluation identified 11 that obtained substantial results, and 4 had a weak performance. The remaining nine did not address the issue.

Assistance with computerizing municipal accounts was the tool most often used to improve municipalities' financial management. Smaller and more remote municipalities in many countries—Chile, The Gambia, Georgia, Tanzania, and Tamil Nadu State (India), for instance—adopted computerized accounting thanks to technical assistance and training packages offered by their respective MDPs. Software and hardware packages were generally provided by local commercial firms that were familiar with local conditions and able to provide the service in the local language. In most cases, municipalities were able to meet national standards of municipal financial reporting— requiring municipal financial information to be available in real time—promoted by their country's Ministry of Finance.

Where training was more intense—for instance, with more than 35 courses in double-entry accounting under **India II** in Tamil Nadu and with plenty of places for municipal applicants available through **The Gambia MDP**—account modernization was successful. Through technical assistance at the central and local levels, **Tanzania I** ensured that all municipalities participating in the project had—and still have today—up-to-date and audited municipal accounts. This was not the case before the project, or for most other municipalities still, according to the government.

Some very large municipalities took well to modernizing their accounting through MDPs. For instance, under **China III,** the mega-municipality of Tianjin was able to integrate different financial information systems, using the project-supported expansion of its computer network. **Russia IV** helped Kazan make municipal accounts more transparent and strengthened municipal management. It did this by helping unify municipal accounts, introducing standard financial indicators, and making projections to establish performance targets. This was achieved not through standard contracts with consultant providers of technical assistance, but through intensive

Table 4.1: Summary of MDP Results in Municipal Finance

Country	MDP	Project name	Overall outcome of project	Results in—			
				Financial management	Mobilizing revenues	Access to credit	Private finance
Sub-Saharan Africa							
Gambia, The		Poverty Allev. & Cap. Building	M Sat	√	√	—	—
Ghana	I	Second Urban	Sat	√	*	—	—
Mozambique	I	Local Govt. Reform	Unsat	√	*	—	—
Tanzania	I	Urban Sector Rehabilitation	Sat	√	√	—	—
Zimbabwe		Urban Sector & Regional Dev.	M Sat	—	*	—	*
East Asia and Pacific							
China	III	Tianjin Urban Development	Sat	√	—	—	—
China	IV	Zhejiang Multicities Dev.	Sat	—	—	—	—
China	VII	Shanghai Environment	Sat	—	—	—	—
Indonesia	II	East Java/Bali Urban Dev.	M Sat	√	√	—	—
Indonesia	VI	Second East Java Urban Dev.	M Unsat	√	*	—	—
Indonesia	IX	Municipal Innovations	Sat	*	*	—	*
Europe and Central Asia							
Georgia	I	Municipal Infrastructure Rehab.	M Unsat	—	—	—	—
Georgia	II	Mun. Dev. & Decentralization	M Sat	*	√	*	—
Georgia	III	Second Mun. Dev. & Decentral.	Sat	√	√	√	—
Russian Federation	IV	Kazan Municipal Dev.	H Sat	√	√	—	*
Uzbekistan		Tashkent Solid Waste Mgt.	Sat	*	*	—	*
Latin America and the Caribbean							
Brazil	II	Ceará Urban Dev./Water Res.	M Sat	—	*	√	—
Chile	II	Second Municipal Dev.	M Sat	—	*	—	—
Colombia	I	Municipal Dev.	Sat	—	√	√	*
Colombia	IV	Urban Infras Services Dev.	Sat	—	√	√	√
Middle East and North Africa							
Tunisia	I	Municipal Sector Investment	Sat	√	√	√	—
South Asia							
India	I	Tamil Nadu Urban Dev.	M Sat	*	√	*	*
India	II	Tamil Nadu Second Urban Dev.	Sat	√	√	√	—
Sri Lanka		Colombo Env. Improvement	Unsat	—	—	—	—

Sources: IEG PPARs.

Note: Bold = MDPs focused on finance; √ = substantial or higher achievement of element; * = element tackled but with modest or lower achievement; — = element not attempted. (Roman numerals are attached to MDPs in their sequence in the portfolio of 190 operations, dispensed with altogether when there is only one MDP in a particular country.) MDP = municipal development project. **Ratings:** H Sat = highly satisfactory; Sat = satisfactory; M Sat = moderately satisfactory; M Unsat = moderately unsatisfactory; Unsat = unsatisfactory.

interchanges between municipal officials and Bank staff and consultants during the frequent Bank project supervision missions to the city.

The municipality of Maputo in Mozambique was able to unify its accounts in a similar way, thanks to later operations, **Mozambique II** and **III.**

Progress in systemizing municipal accounts was slower under **Georgia II,** where computing skills were in short supply among the weak municipal administrations; this shortcoming was slowly overcome by the follow-on **Georgia III.** Under the **Uzbekistan MDP,** progress was slow in modernizing the accounts and financial information systems of a financially stressed municipal solid waste utility that had little experience with autonomous financial management. These results show that a minimal existing capacity is a precondition for MDPs to obtain substantial results in strengthening financial management.

Mobilizing Own Revenues

Municipalities' own revenues, levied through local taxes, user fees, and charges, have been observed to account for up to one-half of all municipal revenues (Shah 2006). Most of the remainder comes from transfers from higher-level governments.[1] Because such fiscal transfers are usually beyond the control of a municipal-level recipient, the Bank generally supports their reform through Development Policy Lending. MDP reform efforts instead have generally focused on strengthening own-revenue mobilization, which is more amenable to improvement through MDP project assistance (table 4.1).

Eleven of the 24 PPAR MDPs achieved substantial results in revenue mobilization, eight MDP efforts yielded weaker results, and five did not focus on this. Successful MDPs updated tax records, expanded the coverage of cadastres or land registers, and enhanced collections.[2] Important factors contributing to the positive results were MDP incentives that required municipalities to raise revenues to remain eligible for project investment funding.

Factors leading to weaker results included revenues from other sources readily available to municipalities and lack of municipal control over parameters of local tax rates and collections. MDP technical assistance to the municipalities (with tight oversight by capable higher-level authorities for wholesale MDPs) helped the municipalities both update their tax rolls and monitor and follow up with delinquent taxpayers. Technical assistance worked well in these cases when it was a condition of municipal access to MDP credit for popular infrastructure.

Municipalities participating in **Colombia I,** for instance, saw their own revenues increase more rapidly than revenues from fiscal transfers over

the 1991–2001 life of the project. More recent reviews of the follow-on projects underscore that the strong revenue performance is continuing. Large individual municipal clients of **India I,** such as Madurai (population 909,908) and Tiruchirapalli (population 775,484), significantly increased their own revenues, enabling them to finance more infrastructure investments from their own resources.

Pointing to positive effects of project incentives and technical assistance, **Georgia II** participant municipalities' own revenues grew by 11 percent during 1998–2002, but those of nonparticipants fell by 16 percent. Under **Georgia III,** own revenues of the 11 participant municipalities continued to grow by 58 percent from 2002 to 2005; nonparticipants saw their revenues rise by only 35 percent.

Although such large figures may be the result of increases from a very low base, more important for an evaluation is the assessment of the differences between the performance of municipalities that participated in an MDP and the performance of those that did not. Although details are scarce, **Indonesia II** did report enhanced revenue collection among the 45 municipalities assisted by the project in East Java and Bali. **The Gambia's MDP** also reported good results, as own revenues of participating municipalities grew by 9 percent annually, well above the 5–6 percent target the MDP set for them. **Tanzania I** enabled municipalities to more than double their own revenues over the project period with the help of modern computer mapping and accounting.

Through **Russia IV,** Kazan municipality was particularly successful in increasing its own revenues. It had a particularly important and urgent reason to do so. Following the establishment of the new autonomous Kazan municipal authority in 2004, existing large federal transfers were slated to be cut and had to be replaced quickly. The effect was similar to that of a fiscal shock, although not unexpected. The MDP helped Kazan municipality find alternative sources of revenue, a task it did well, taking municipal finances into surplus by mid-2007 after a succession of deficits.

Tunisia I produced excellent results as well that continue, more than eight years after implementation completion. Not only did MDP-participating municipalities there increase their own revenues more than other municipalities, but the participants produced surpluses that were twice the size targeted. These results show that important achievements in financial performance can be obtained both through wholesale and retail models of MDPs.

In two MDPs—**Ghana I** and **Chile II**—municipal clients increased their own revenues, but the growth could not be attributed to the projects. Other municipalities that did not participate in the projects enjoyed similar increases, caused by buoyant macroeconomic growth exogenous to the operations. In such cases, it is important not to mistakenly read project success into the results. Indeed, questions still need to be asked about what more the MDPs could have done to help client municipalities achieve a better revenue performance than nonparticipants. In the cases of **Brazil II, Indonesia VII, Mozambique I,** and the **Zimbabwe MDP,** results in raising more own revenues were weak where some municipalities were reluctant to raise taxes further.

Instead of looking broadly at improving municipal revenues overall, the **Uzbekistan MDP** concentrated on stimulating direct cost recovery from the project investments themselves; the results were only modest. In this case, the municipality of Tashkent allowed necessary annual adjustments to the solid waste tariff to lapse for four years, undermining the sustainability of the service; a last-minute adjustment did throw a financial lifeline to the system operator. In some other countries, notably China and Sri Lanka, increasing local revenues, whether through MDPs or by other means, simply was not a priority for the national government.

Municipal Creditworthiness and Debt Management

Through offering lines of credit for financing investments in infrastructure and municipal services, some wholesale MDPs were able to introduce many municipalities to borrowing on a significant scale. The metaphor of "bringing municipalities to market" through direct borrowing or issuing bonds appeals to the rigor such commitments impose on financial management, as municipalities service their debts and seek to remain creditworthy.[3] Exposure to credit and its accompanying opportunities and risks forged a new approach to municipal finance in some cities.

Six of the eight MDPs reviewed by PPARs that were focused on strengthened municipal access to credit yielded substantial results. An important factor in these positive outcomes was the MDP itself making resources available to municipalities that became creditworthy. One other MDP tried but failed to bring municipalities to market because the availability of other grant funding undermined their demand for credit. The remaining 16 MDPs set no target for themselves in this area (table 4.1). Retail MDPs had too few municipal clients to start credit markets, which generally require a large number of municipalities to be functional.

On the positive side, several small municipalities learned about servicing and paying off debt for the first time under **Brazil II** in Ceará State. **Colombia I** and **IV,** successive wholesale MDPs, both helped bring municipalities to market as intended by introducing 179 of them to credit operations for the first time. These municipalities remain engaged today. Under these projects Colombia's national Local Development Fund, FINDETER, currently with a AAA Fitch credit rating, stimulated the supply of private credit to municipalities. It did this by rediscounting commercial bank loans to them for financing infrastructure and municipal services; that enabled the successful consolidation of a new local credit market. Furthermore, the operations fostered a municipal culture of creditworthiness that was publicly monitored by international credit-rating agencies that set up local operations in the country.

Eight municipalities were awarded a BBB or higher credit rating, which in Colombia is regarded as being equivalent to investment grade. Through **Colombia I,** the municipality of Pereira (population 440,000), with an A+ Fitch credit rating, went one step further: in 1998 it successfully issued municipal bonds that were heavily oversubscribed in the local market. This rich experience also revealed possible market constraints on the demand side, however. Even when creditworthy, several municipalities in Colombia were reluctant to assume debt for municipal services. Their leaders were cautious about borrowing and their constituents seemingly satisfied with the existing levels of local services provided.

Local credit markets in other countries have been stimulated by other Bank-financed MDPs. **India II** encouraged municipalities in Tamil Nadu to become creditworthy to have better access to loans awarded by the Tamil Nadu Urban Development Fund. The state's second largest city, Madurai, went one credit step further. With the project's technical assistance, the municipality issued bonds to raise funds to pay for the construction of an inner ring road. But these successes were built on the back of shortcomings of the earlier **India I,** which made little progress with municipal credit. Concessional state-level grant financing continued to be the major source of revenue for municipalities, far outstripping resources coming through the MDP's line of credit.

Some progress, albeit modest and very protracted, has been made toward establishing the building blocks of municipal credit systems in Georgia. **Georgia III** helped make the country's nine largest municipalities creditworthy—at least in the eyes of the official Municipal Development Fund of Georgia. This was the first time this had been accomplished in that country's history and was a necessary step toward a financial market recognition of municipal creditworthiness. In both countries—Georgia and India—several municipalities took out loans for the first time to finance services and infrastructure, learning quickly how to properly manage a debt portfolio.

Downside foreign exchange risks, especially volatile at the end of 2008, have rarely been treated openly in the designs of MDPs. Nor have they been found to constrain municipal credit. But the consequences of sharp local currency devaluations in several countries have laid bare the question of who should be responsible for the additional local currency payment needed to amortize a foreign currency-denominated debt. Standard MDP practice has been for the borrower, usually the central government financial intermediary, to take this risk, part of which it may be able to price into the credit offered to municipalities. Municipalities, after all, are rarely foreign currency earners.

Under **Colombia I** and **II,** FINDETER itself was able manage this risk professionally through forward pricing of foreign currencies and also by maintaining foreign account holdings, ensuring that its own exposure did not exceed more than 12.7 percent of its total liabilities. Meanwhile, Colombian municipalities were shielded from that risk. **India II** took a similar approach, expecting the state-level Tamil Nadu Urban Development Fund to manage the foreign exchange risks. It moved more cautiously, however, given that fewer hedging instruments were available in that country's financial markets.

One MDP also provided temporary relief to a municipality that was hard pressed by short-term debt that an earlier municipal administration had left unpaid. **Colombia IV,** through advice on portfolio management, helped the large municipality of Barranquilla (population 1.4 million) pay off all its short-term debts, accumulated during the 1990s, by the year 2001.

Several questions about providing credit to municipalities remain, however. Should lending conditions between public sector agencies try to simulate exactly what the market would itself prescribe? Do municipal credit markets in developing countries that are controlled or tightly regulated by government agencies provide accurate pricing signals on interest rates, terms of repayment, and other lending conditions? The Levy Report to the Bank (World Bank 1989) and the subsequent 1998 Operational Policy 8.30 on financial intermediary lending tended toward negative answers to these questions. This discouraged earmarked lending, such as credit to municipalities, which was thought to fragment broader financial markets and undermine their efficiency. A recent study by the Bank's Urban Anchor argued that this kind of lending to municipalities could effectively improve service delivery when the MDP is deliberately adapted to the needs of its municipal clients (Annez, Huet, and Peterson 2008).

Private Finance Participation

MDP incursions into enabling and stimulating private finance of municipal services have yielded few positive results. The focus of the 24 MDPs reviewed by PPARs on this aspect of municipal management was very weak. To seriously engage the private sector, municipalities have to build teams of experts to prepare and supervise contract management units, something that many still lack.

Just seven projects addressed this, and only one obtained substantial efficacy in achieving greater private finance (table 4.1). This was under **Colombia IV,** which helped municipalities increase water, gas, and solid waste tariffs, thereby making some services profitable for private investors for the first time. At the same time it made some services less affordable to the poor because it did not provide a corresponding safety net for them. Average household expenditure on basic sanitation in Colombia rose by 204 percent between 1997 and 2003. Thus, an important factor in this positive result was the ability and willingness of municipalities to increase local tariffs, albeit with some loss of affordability.

Factors undermining successful private financing are mostly related to private investors hesitating to participate in the face of pricing or regulatory uncertainties. Thus, land development for low-income families by private developers under **India I** did not go far, as the developers showed little interest in the scheme, again for pricing

reasons. Privatizing the loss-making municipal solid waste management operation in the **Uzbekistan MDP,** a specific aim of the European Bank for Reconstruction and Development, the Bank's partner in the project, did not proceed because of lack of interest by private investors.

The planned privatization of the municipal water utility in Kazan, supported by the Bank under **Russia IV,** did not go far because the European Bank for Reconstruction and Development (not partnering with the Bank in this operation) sought to strengthen the existing public sector operator instead. The **Zimbabwe MDP's** hope of stimulating private finance of municipal housing was frustrated by private building societies' own financial weaknesses, which arose from their inability to compete with postal savings and their inability to provide an affordable product for the needs of lower- and middle-income households. In hindsight, a more thorough analysis of Zimbabwe's housing market would not have recommended pursuing this objective. Under **Indonesia IX,** private financing of local municipal markets or other infrastructure did not appear on the scale hoped for, as small municipalities especially were unable to articulate a regulatory framework for the local investors.

The limited results in securing private finance for local services point to several areas in which MDP design should be strengthened: accurate analysis of local financial markets, a realistic assessment of the demand for such services at the prices they will be offered, and, most important, an assurance of a reasonable chance of some profit. In addition, it is important for an MDP appraisal to affirm that municipalities understand their responsibilities in relation to the regulatory framework, especially for pricing that would govern such private finance.

Chapter 5

Evaluation Highlights

- Although all 190 MDPs focused on municipal service provision, less than one-third used cost-benefit analysis for evaluating or prioritizing investments.
- More than one-third of the evaluated MDPs were able to substantially help municipalities manage procurement for the first time.
- Most MDPs paid little attention to O&M, significantly increasing the risk to development outcomes.
- Few MDPs focused explicitly on improving the lives of the poor, and evidence of actual results of better access to services obtained is thin.

Municipal solid waste disposal in Tashkent, Uzbekistan. Photo courtesy of Roy Gilbert.

Managing Service Provision

This chapter reports the findings of IEG assessments of the efficacy of the following elements of managing service provision: prioritizing investments through cost-benefit analysis, conducting procurement for service investments, and handling the O&M of ongoing services.

Elements of Service Provision

Prioritizing investments in service provision

When resources are scarce, municipal managers need to know, at the outset, the best options for investment and how well those investments perform at completion. To help them, the Bank requires MDPs, like other investment operations it finances, to conduct ex ante and ex post economic evaluations of investment performance. The present study found, however, that only 7 of the 24 PPAR MDPs did this effectively. Those seven applied the instrument of choice, a cost-benefit analysis that yielded an economic rate of return (ERR) or an estimate of the net present value, at appraisal and/or completion (table 5.1).

Project documentation of the remaining MDPs gave diverse reasons for the lack of economic analysis. The reasons included the high cost of estimating ERRs, the complexities of measuring external costs and benefits, and the exempt status of some MDPs because of their quasi-emergency status. Nevertheless, seven MDPs facing challenges such as these were able to successfully assess their efficiency through ERR estimates.

Most of these MDPs applied simple models of cost-benefit analysis that used available data,

notably data produced by project M&E. **Ghana I** made simple but methodologically robust estimates that did not require a lot of data. The project's municipal slum upgrading components in Tamale (population 360,579) yielded an ERR of 29 percent, using benefits derived from the (realistic) increases of land values following project improvements.

Tanzania I applied a similar method, and the **Zimbabwe MDP** incorporated shadow pricing into the assessment. Beyond Africa, **China III, Indonesia II, Georgia III,** and **India I** all saw municipalities themselves directly involved in the ERR work, under the guidance of the MDPs.

Making the investments: Procurement

Through MDPs, many municipalities engaged in competitive tendering for works and supplies for the first time; traditionally that procurement had been in the hands of the central government. From its PPAR assessments in the field, IEG found that local MDP beneficiaries were better informed about service improvements to their neighborhoods when municipalities themselves had carried out the procurement. Nine MDPs reviewed by PPARs across most Regions obtained substantial results in this area mainly by introducing municipalities to procurement management for the first time.

Table 5.1: Summary of MDP Results in Service Provision

Country	MDP	Project name	Overall outcome of project	ERRs	Results in— Procurement	O&M
Sub-Saharan Africa						
Gambia, The		**Pov. Allev. & Capacity Building**	M Sat	*	*	√
Ghana	I	**Second Urban Project**	Sat	√	*	√
Mozambique	I	**Local Govt. Reform**	Unsat	—	*	—
Tanzania	I	**Urban Sector Rehabilitation**	Sat	√	√	√
Zimbabwe		**Urban Sector & Regional Dev.**	M Sat	√	*	*
East Asia and Pacific						
China	III	**Tianjin Urban Development**	Sat	√	√	*
China	IV	**Zhejiang Multicities Dev.**	Sat	*	*	—
China	VII	**Shanghai Environment**	Sat	—	*	—
Indonesia	II	**East Java/Bali Urban Dev.**	M Sat	√	*	*
Indonesia	VI	**Second East Java Urban Dev.**	M Unsat	*	*	*
Indonesia	IX	**Municipal Innovations**	Sat	—	*	—
Europe and Central Asia						
Georgia	I	**Mun. Infrastructure Rehab.**	M Unsat	—	—	*
Georgia	II	**Mun. Dev. & Decentralization**	M Sat	—	—	*
Georgia	III	**Second Mun. Dev. & Decentral.**	Sat	√	√	*
Russian Federation	IV	**Kazan Municipal Dev.**	H Sat	*	√	*
Uzbekistan		**Tashkent Solid Waste Mgt.**	Sat	*	√	*
Latin America and the Caribbean						
Brazil	II	**Ceará Urban Dev. & Water Res.**	M Sat	*	√	—
Chile	II	**Second Municipal Dev.**	M Sat	—	—	*
Colombia	I	**Municipal Dev.**	Sat	*	√	*
Colombia	IV	**Urban Infras. Services Dev.**	Sat	—	√	*
Middle East and North Africa						
Tunisia	I	**Municipal Sector Investment**	Sat	—	*	√
South Asia						
India	I	**Tamil Nadu Urban Dev.**	M Sat	√	*	—
India	II	**Tamil Nadu Second Urban Dev.**	Sat	*	*	*
Sri Lanka		**Colombo Env. Improvement**	Unsat	—	√	—

Sources: IEG PPARs.

Note: Bold = MDPs focused on service provision; √ = substantial or higher achievement of element; * = element tackled but with modest or lower achievement; — = element not attempted. In the case of ERRs, achievements are rated according to the use made of the tool itself, not according to the value of the estimated rate of return. (Roman numerals are attached to MDPs in their sequence in the portfolio of 190 operations, dispensed with altogether when there is only one MDP in a particular country.) ERR = economic rate of return; MDP = municipal development project; O&M = operations and maintenance. **Ratings:** H Sat = highly satisfactory; Sat = satisfactory; M Sat = moderately satisfactory; M Unsat = moderately unsatisfactory; Unsat = unsatisfactory.

In other cases, particularly in East Asia and Pacific and South Asia, the *impact* of MDPs on procurement practice was less. But this does not mean that they all failed. Several larger municipalities already had experience with procurement and continued to handle it proficiently, as they had done before an MDP whose design rightly did not focus unduly on this issue (table 5.1).

For example, **Brazil II** enabled 49 mostly small municipalities such as Quixadá (population 49,328) in Ceará State to oversee competitive procurement of works for upgrading low-income neighborhoods for the first time. At the opposite end of the scale, a very large municipality, such as Tianjin under **China III,** became quite expert in conducting complex international competitive bidding after its purchase of sophisticated traffic monitoring equipment for the city and state-of-the-art equipment for the solid waste disposal site at Shuangkou. These became a model for all of China.

The experience of **Russia IV** convinced Kazan municipality that Bank-standard local competitive procurement procedures helped it obtain lower prices. Kazan thus decided to apply these procedures voluntarily to urban street upgrades financed from its own budget. This practice continues today, though the project has closed. Previously, Kazan had relied on sole-source acquisitions, typical of former Soviet practices, which the MDP helped reform. Although municipalities themselves drive such results, for the most part they have to be consistent with national or higher-level legislation.

O&M of services

For their own investments and for those made by others within their jurisdictions, municipalities are generally responsible for the use and upkeep of the assets provided by MDPs. Past urban development projects in which central government authorities simply delivered infrastructure assets to a city without involving or sometimes even consulting the municipality about O&M generally failed for lack of municipal ownership (IEG 2004, p. 18).

By putting municipalities at center stage, MDPs make municipal O&M responsibilities clearer. They also provide both challenges and opportunities for local administrations to ensure that urban infrastructure continues to provide good-quality services and benefits to users. It is clear that many municipalities have yet to rise to this challenge. This study found only four MDPs that achieved substantial results in strengthening the

municipal management of O&M. In the remainder of the cases, O&M was either disregarded by MDPs that focused primarily on supporting the initial service investment, or it did not succeed for lack of funding (table 5.1).

On the positive side, **Tanzania I** successfully introduced computerized maintenance systems to 10 municipalities that used them to track and plan the maintenance of urban streets. Although budget shortfalls are often given as a reason for the lack of O&M, **The Gambia MDP** helped nine municipalities, home to half the country's urban population, to establish O&M accounts that were adequately funded by the municipalities themselves. Although quite an achievement in itself, local administrations still lacked the necessary equipment and technical and managerial capacity to carry out all the maintenance needed.

Better results were obtained through **Ghana I,** which even introduced parking controls in the central areas of the cities of Accra (population 2.0 million) and Sekondi-Takoradi (population 371,791) to facilitate street cleaning and access by maintenance vehicles. Under **Tunisia I,** the remote municipality of Kasserine (population 82,000) upgraded its Ezzouhour district, keeping it in good condition through careful maintenance, sometimes with the help of the local residents.

Inadequate attention to O&M led to negative project results for MDPs. Insufficient O&M funding meant, for instance, that the municipality of Bulawayo (population 699,000) under the **Zimbabwe MDP** could not pay for the pumping needed to keep the project's Nkulumane sewage plant operating. Similarly, under **Indonesia II,** a water supply system for the Kintamani district of Denpasar (population 405,923), Bali, fell into disuse because the municipality could afford to operate the pumps for only a fraction of the time needed each day. Other municipalities in East Java were able to conduct everyday maintenance such as patching minor pavement failures, but not heavier repairs. Even prosperous municipalities may feel that incentives are not right to encourage

O&M. Under **Tunisia I,** for example, officials of Ariana (population 237,395) felt that it was better to neglect routine maintenance in upgraded areas and allow the infrastructure to fail, because that increased the chance that the government would finance a complete replacement.

Sectors Most Affected and Service Quality

IEG PPARs show that MDPs cover a wide spectrum of municipal services in their efforts to strengthen municipal management: upgrading existing infrastructure, providing new assets, and improving the operation of existing infrastructure. MDPs typically supported improvements to urban road and street paving, drainage and lighting, basic sanitation, solid waste and slum upgrading, environmental improvements, transport, and others. By convention, Bank support for important municipal education and health services has been provided through dedicated sectoral projects, not through MDPs. By mandate, Bank assistance has generally not been involved with the important political and security work that municipalities in many countries carry out.

Street paving and drainage were the most popular municipal services supported by MDP management strengthening in Colombia, Ghana, India, and Georgia. **Colombia IV** helped improve the urban environment of low-income peripheral areas of several cities, improvements that are still being maintained. Paving streets reduced dust during dry seasons, and better drainage avoided repeat flooding and impassable streets during rainy seasons.

Ghana I radically transformed the central areas of Accra and Sekondi-Takoradi through street paving and drainage, especially in places where street markets were held daily. This improved access to markets, whose stallholders reported increased business. The upgraded locations made the cleanup after the markets easier, too, thereby improving the urban environment. **Georgia's** three MDPs improved residential neighborhoods by paving streets.

Neighborhood upgrading and basic sanitation took MDP support for services one step further by introducing water and sewer services into poor neighborhoods. The large scale of service provision across Tamil Nadu by **India I** is evident from the upgrading of 489 slums. Through the upgrade, 76,000 people gained better access to their homes and businesses through paved footpaths and proper drainage. These improvements were implemented across 35 municipalities that participated directly for the first time in providing such better-quality services. **India II** continued to provide more of the same in 102 additional municipalities, where sample beneficiary assessments point to better-quality basic sanitation services.

Tanzania I helped the smaller municipalities of Mororgoro (population 251,000) and Tabora (population 145,000) significantly reduce unaccounted-for water by helping to repair leaky main lines. Consumers reported that water became available for more hours per day than before the project. Unaccounted-for water continued to be a problem in some **Colombia I** municipalities, however, where network coverage was extended without achieving overall system improvements.

When trying to offer large-scale sewage treatment plants through MDPs, municipalities had more limited success. Investment cost overruns and high operating costs put them out of the reach of municipal finances and resulted in incomplete and nonoperational plants, as in the municipality of Tema (population 155,782) under **Ghana I** and in the Nkulumane district of Bulawayo under **Zimbabwe's MDP.** The innovative introduction of a low-cost, small-scale *modular* approach to sewage treatment by the municipality of Malang (population 747,000) through **Indonesia VI** also has met with little success. Beneficiaries continue to discharge sewage into storm drains, rather than paying the (modest) fee imposed by the new system.

MDPs provided basic sanitation through solid waste management, too, with generally positive results. **China III** led to the building and operation of the country's first sanitary landfill at Shuangkou near Tianjin. Similar solid waste disposal solutions were offered through MDPs in **Sri Lanka, Uzbekistan,** and **Tanzania.** Although they did not fully meet all the ambitious performance standards set for them, the MDP solutions do represent significant advances over previous practices of uncontrolled dumping. Solid waste collection equipment and technical assistance provided through **Tanzania I,** for instance, raised the share of garbage produced that was actually collected from 40 percent across the 9 cities to 55 percent, a significant improvement in service quality and benefit for the urban environment. In the **Uzbekistan MDP,** the quality of solid waste collection improved through more regular pickups at controlled collection points rather than through an increase in the quantity collected.

In one case, a large number of municipalities benefited. **Colombia I's** help to 179 municipalities had an impact on service levels that made its mark on indicators at the national level. Between 1993 and 2003, when the project was implemented, basic sanitation coverage of the lowest quintile of Colombia's population in income distribution rose from 77 percent to 83 percent.

Environmental improvements by MDPs beyond those resulting from street paving and basic sanitation included both long-term and short-term provision of other services. Through **Sri Lanka's MDP,** the municipality of Colombo (population 2.3 million) sought to reduce the pollution of the city's Beira Lake, but with limited demonstrable results. A significant short-term environmental gain was made by **China VII,** however. The project enabled the Shanghai municipality (population 14.6 million) to build a large water catchment plant on the upper, less-polluted reaches of the environmentally stressed Huangpo River. Today, more than five years after completion, the plant continues to provide safe drinking water to more than 8 million consumers, whose health had been seriously at risk from the poor water quality of the old intake.

Other municipal services were mostly in the area of urban transport. **China III** introduced better traffic surveillance and monitoring to the megacity of Tianjin, although without giving much higher priority to public transport. **India I** in Tamil Nadu, however, brought considerable improvements to the quality of the bus service in the state capital Chennai (population 4.3 million) through the purchase of new bus chassis. Bus transport was a key feature, too, of **Tanzania I,** which upgraded municipal bus terminals in eight municipalities, providing paved areas for buses and covered shelters for passengers. The terminals became hives of commercial activity and are still booming today, in addition to handling 50 percent more buses than before the project. A special MDP transport improvement came through **Georgia I,** which provided spare parts to enable the Metro system of the capital Tbilisi to continue operations after supplies had been interrupted following the collapse of the Soviet Union.

Income Levels of Beneficiaries— Poverty Reduction

Better municipal management of service delivery could benefit all income groups of the population living and working within the jurisdiction of a municipality. But does it bring benefits to the poor and reduce poverty?

Only 27 percent of the 190 MDPs in the portfolio explicitly aimed to bring municipal services to the poor. Evidence of actual results achieved by the 114 completed MDPs is patchy, at best. There is some evidence that MDPs benefitted the poor, but it is thin, which is to be expected from an MDP portfolio so little focused on poverty. Only 4 of the 24 PPAR MDPs had project objectives explicitly aimed at improving the lives of the poor: **Brazil II, Ghana I, The Gambia,** and **Tanzania I.** A few others, such as **Colombia I** and **II** and **Indonesia VI,** introduced basic sanitation to poorer districts of client municipalities, even though their formal objective statements did not specify a focus on the poor.

IEG field inspections confirmed that basic municipal services provided through **Brazil II** in

Ceará State had indeed benefited poor districts of what were mostly low-income municipalities in this poor northeastern region of the country. **The Gambia MDP,** with poverty alleviation in the project title, benefited more poor, unskilled construction workers than targeted, albeit only temporarily through construction work arising directly from the project implementation. **Tanzania I** brought urgent relief to some 13,600 poor residents of Dar es Salaam (population 2.8 million) through drilling 34 emergency boreholes (serving 400 people each) during a drought emergency. **Ghana I** successfully introduced basic sanitation, street paving, and lighting to 24,000 poor people living in the Ashaiman squatter district of Tema, in the port city of Accra.

The poverty results of these operations are themselves worth further scrutiny by those who wish to emulate such results in future operations. Indeed, the evidence showing the lack of poverty focus of most MDPs points to a clear need to report the results of such experiences much more thoroughly.

Implementation Completion Reports rarely provide information about the income levels of MDP beneficiaries. If future MDPs are to benefit the poor on a larger scale and are to be seen doing so, they will have to do two things. First, they need to sharpen the focus of their objectives on helping the poor, making it explicit in project objective statements and in project design. A more poverty-oriented approach would explain, for instance, how the poor would benefit from municipal investments and services rendered better through MDP municipal management strengthening.

Second, they need to harness M&E so that the design of these systems helps establish clear goals for poverty alleviation and so that M&E implementation shows exactly what has been achieved. As noted earlier, there is much work still to do in this area for the Bank to fully deploy its poverty reduction mission through its partner municipalities. Being able to assess poverty-related objectives and project design, as well as actual results of MDPs, would be an important contribution.

Chapter 6

Community life resumes for newly resettled residents of Ningbo, China. Photo courtesy of Roy Gilbert.

Conclusions

With cities now home to more than half the world's population and providing the majority of world gross domestic product, improving municipal management is crucial for development. The Bank's chosen instrument to support this has been the MDP, 190 of which have assisted nearly 3,000 municipalities in 76 countries worldwide over the past decade.

IEG field assessments of 24 completed MDPs, desk reviews of 90 more, and an overview of 76 ongoing operations have highlighted the strengths and weaknesses of these operations, which are aimed at helping municipalities strengthen their management in the planning, finance, and service provision dimensions. This study has found positive MDP experiences worth emulation, as well as weaker results that point to areas in need of improvement. The following forward-looking lessons may help strengthen municipal management.

- Among the three dimensions of municipal management—planning, finance, and service provision—MDP support for strengthening municipal finance most often yielded successful results. The Bank should continue to support tightened municipal financial management, municipalities raising their own revenues, and municipalities being brought to local credit markets when conditions are appropriate.
- Project documentation that routinely reports basic data about each client (municipality name, population, and MDP investment) is vital to developing a better understanding of the scope of MDP results.
- Wholesale MDPs have yielded better outcomes than retail MDPs over the past decade, but more analysis is needed to understand the precise reasons for the performance differen-

tial. Retail MDPs might perform better if they incorporated more of the winning elements of wholesale MDPs, such as performance-based incentives and a focus on finance.

- More frequent use of cost-benefit or cost-effectiveness analysis would help MDPs' municipal clients select the best investments and achieve better outcomes. IEG found that only half of the 114 completed MDPs did this, with the best coverage in the Sub-Saharan Africa Region.
- For M&E to succeed in MDPs, it has to be useful and not unduly burdensome to municipalities themselves; it must also keep a focus on achieving results, particularly for the poor. Strong M&E can also help reduce the expense of cost-benefit analyses by providing some of the data needed to estimate ERRs. Few MDPs have succeeded with this.
- Private finance of municipal services can be encouraged through better analysis of demand and of local financial markets. Stable regulations also help municipalities gain the trust of private investors.
- Thus far, little evidence exists that stronger municipal management has benefited the poor. MDPs need to give much more attention to poverty reduction in defining MDP objectives, showing how the poor would benefit from municipal investments and services improved through stronger municipal management.

Appendixes

Project ID	MDP	Type	Project name	Period[a]	Commitment US$ millions	Outcome	Bank performance	Borrower performance
Sub-Saharan Africa								
P000097	Benin I	R	Urban Rehabilitation & Management	1992–98	23	H Sat	H Sat	Sat
P035648	Benin II	R	First Decentralized City Management	1999–2005	26	Sat	Sat	H Sat
P082725	Benin III	R	Second Decentralized City Management	2006–	35	—	—	—
P000297	Burkina Faso I	R	Urban Environment	1995–2005	37	Sat	Sat	Sat
P084027	Burkina Faso II	R	Decentralized Urban Capacity Building	2007–	10	—	—	—
P064961	Burundi	W	Public Works & Employment Creation	2001–	40	—	—	—
P084002	Cameroon	R	Urban & Water Development Support	2007–	80	—	—	—
P072030	Chad	R	Urban Development	2007–	15	—	—	—
P037575	Côte d'Ivoire	W	Municipal Support	1995–2004	40	Unsat	Unsat	Unsat
P000712	Ethiopia I	R	Second Addis Urban Development	1990–99	35	Unsat	Sat	Unsat
P050938	Ethiopia II	W	Capacity Building for Decentralized Service Delivery	2003–	26	—	—	—
P074020	Ethiopia III	R	Public Sector Capacity Building	2004–	100	—	—	—
P101473	Ethiopia IV	R	Urban Water Supply & Sanitation	2007–	100	—	—	—
P057997	Gambia, The	R	Poverty Alleviation & Capacity Building	1999–2007	15	M Sat	Sat	Sat
P000910	Ghana I	R	Second Urban	1990–99	70	Sat	Sat	Sat
P000936	Ghana II	W	Local Govt. Development	1994–2003	39	Sat	Sat	Sat
P000973	Ghana III	R	Urban Environment & Sanitation	1996–2004	71	M Sat	Unsat	Unsat
P050624	Ghana IV	W	Fifth Urban	2000–04	11	Sat	Sat	Sat
P001074	Guinea I	R	Third Urban Development (APL)	1999–2005	18	Sat	Sat	Sat
P091297	Guinea II	R	Third Urban (Phase 2)	2008–	15	—	—	—
P001319	Kenya	R	Urban Transport	1996–2005	115	M Unsat	Unsat	Unsat
P001512	Madagascar I	R	Antananarivo Plain Development	1990–2000	31	M Unsat	Unsat	Unsat
P001583	Madagascar II	R	Antananarivo Urban Works Pilot	1994–99	18	Sat	Sat	Sat
P048697	Madagascar III	R	Urban Infrastructure	1997–2005	35	Sat	Sat	Sat
P001636	Malawi	R	Local Govt. Development	1992–2001	24	M Unsat	Unsat	Unsat
P001750	Mali I	R	Urban Development & Decentralization	1997–2005	80	M Unsat	Sat	Unsat
P090075	Mali II	R	Second Transport Sector	2007–	90	—	—	—
P034106	Mauritania I	W	Urban Infrastructure & Pilot Decentralization	1996–2002	14	Sat	Sat	Sat
P069095	Mauritania II	R	Urban Development Program	2002–	70	—	—	—
P001791	Mozambique I	R	Local Govt. Reform & Engineering	1993–99	23	Unsat	H Unsat	H Unsat

(Continues on the next page.)

Project ID	MDP	Type	Project name	Period[a]	Commitment US$ millions	Outcome	Bank performance	Borrower performance
Sub-Saharan Africa (continued)								
P001806	Mozambique II	W	Municipal Development	2002–07	34	M Sat	M Sat	M Sat
P096332	Mozambique III	R	Maputo Municipal Development Program	2007–	30	—	—	—
P049691	Niger I	W	Urban Infrastructure Rehabilitation	1997–2003	20	Sat	Sat	Sat
P095949	Niger II	R	Local Urban Infrastructure Development	2008–	—	—	—	—
P002074	Nigeria I	R	Oyo State Urban	1990–99	50	Unsat	Sat	Unsat
P071340	Nigeria II	R	Lagos Metropolitan Development & Governance	2007–	200	—	—	—
P060005	Rwanda	R	Urban Infrastructure & City Management (APL)	2006–	20	—	—	—
P002365	Senegal I	W	Urban Development & Decentralization Program	1998–2005	75	H Sat	H Sat	Sat
P084022	Senegal II	R	Local Authorities Development Program	2007–	80	—	—	—
P076901	South Africa	W	Municipal Financial Management (TAL)	2003–	15	—	—	—
P002669	Swaziland I	R	Urban Development	1995–2005	29	Sat	Sat	Sat
P095232	Swaziland II	R	Local Government	2008–	—	—	—	—
P002758	Tanzania I	R	Urban Sector Rehabilitation	1996–2005	105	H Sat	Sat	Sat
P070736	Tanzania II	R	Local Govt. Support	2005–	52	—	—	—
P002865	Togo	R	Lome Urban Development	1994–2003	26	Sat	Sat	Unsat
P002933	Uganda I	R	First Urban	1991–2000	29	Sat	Sat	Sat
P059223	Uganda II	R	Nakivubo Channel Rehabilitation	1999–2004	22	Sat	Sat	Sat
P002992	Uganda III	R	Local Govt. Development Program	2000–04	81	Sat	Sat	Sat
P044679	Uganda IV	W	Economic & Financial Management	2000–07	34	Sat	M Sat	M Sat
P078382	Uganda V	R	Kampala Institutional & Infrastructure Development	2008–	34	—	—	—
P003241	Zambia	R	Urban Restructuring	1995–2002	33	M Sat	Sat	Sat
P003294	Zimbabwe	W	Urban Sector & Regional Development	1989–2000	80	M Sat	Sat	Sat
East Asia and Pacific								
P003564	China I	R	Beijing Environment	1992–99	125	M Sat	Sat	Sat
P003565	China II	R	Shanghai Metropolitan Transport	1992–99	60	Sat	Sat	Sat
P003568	China III	R	Tianjin Urban Development	1992–2001	100	Sat	Sat	H Sat
P003473	China IV	R	Zhejiang Multicities Development	1993–2003	110	Sat	Sat	Sat
P003580	China V	R	Southern Jiangsu Environmental Protection	1993–2001	250	M Unsat	Unsat	Unsat
P003622	China VI	R	Second Shanghai Metropolitan Transport	1994–2001	150	Sat	Sat	Sat
P003586	China VII	R	Shanghai Environment	1994–2003	160	Sat	Sat	Sat

P003598	China VIII	R	Liaoning Environment	1995–2004	110	Sat	Sat	Sat	Sat
P003603	China IX	R	Enterprise Housing & Social Security Reform	1995–2005	350	Sat	Sat	Sat	Sat
P003602	China X	R	Hubei Urban Environment	1996–2005	150	M Sat	M Sat	Sat	Sat
P003646	China XI	R	Chongqing Industrial Pollution Control & Reform	1996–2003	170	Unsat	Unsat	Sat	Sat
P003599	China XII	R	Yunnan Environment	1996–2005	150	M Sat	M Sat	Sat	Sat
P040185	China XIII	R	Shandong Environment	1998–2006	95	Sat	Sat	Sat	Sat
P041890	China XIV	R	Liaoning Urban Transport	1999–2006	150	M Sat	M Sat	Sat	Sat
P043933	China XV	R	Sichuan Urban Environment	1999–2007	152	M Sat	M Sat	Sat	M Sat
P049436	China XVI	R	Chongqing Urban Environment	2000–	200	—	—	—	—
P045915	China XVII	R	Urumqi Urban Transport	2001–	100	—	—	—	—
P056596	China XVIII	R	Shijiazhuang Urban Transport	2001–	100	—	—	—	—
P040599	China XIX	R	Tianjin Second Urban Development	2003–	150	—	—	—	—
P069852	China XX	R	Wuhan Urban Transport	2004–	200	—	—	—	—
P081346	China XXI	R	Liuzhou Environment Management	2005–	100	—	—	—	—
P081161	China XXII	W	Chongqing Small Cities Infrastructure Improvement	2005–	180	—	—	—	—
P075732	China XXIII	R	Second Shanghai Urban Environment (APL)	2006–	180	—	—	—	—
P003922	Indonesia I	R	Sulawesi—Irian Jaya Urban Development	1991–99	100	M Sat	Sat	Sat	Sat
P003943	Indonesia II	W	East Java/Bali Urban Development	1991–98	180	M Sat	Sat	Sat	Sat
P003998	Indonesia III	R	Surabaya Urban Development	1994–2001	175	H Unsat	Unsat	Unsat	Unsat
P003890	Indonesia IV	R	Semarang Surakarta Urban Development	1994–2002	174	M Unsat	Sat	Sat	Unsat
P003951	Indonesia V	R	Kalimantan Urban Development	1995–2003	136	Sat	Sat	Sat	Sat
P039312	Indonesia VI	W	Second East Java Urban Development	1996–2002	117	M Unsat	Sat	Sat	Sat
P036053	Indonesia VII	W	Second Sulawesi Urban Development	1997–2003	155	Unsat	Unsat	Unsat	Unsat
P055821	Indonesia VIII	W	Urban Poverty	1999–2004	100	Sat	Sat	Sat	Sat
P056074	Indonesia IX	W	Municipal Innovations	1999–2003	5	Sat	Sat	Sat	Sat
P040528	Indonesia X	R	Western Java Environmental Management	2001–06	17	M Sat	M Sat	Sat	Sat
P072852	Indonesia XI	W	Second Urban Poverty	2002–	100	—	—	—	—
P071296	Indonesia XII	W	Urban Sector Development & Reform	2005–	45	—	—	Sat	Sat
P004175	Korea, Rep. of	R	Pusan Urban Transport	1995–2002	100	M Sat	Sat	Sat	Sat
P036052	Mongolia	R	Urban Services Improvement	1998–2004	17	Sat	Sat	Sat	Sat
P004592	Philippines I	W	Third Municipal Development	1992–2001	68	Sat	Sat	Sat	Sat
P048588	Philippines II	W	Local Govt. Unit Finance & Development	1999–	100	—	—	—	—
P064925	Philippines III	W	Support for Strategic Local Development & Investment	2006–	100	—	—	—	—

(Continues on the next page.)

Project ID	MDP	Type	Project name	Period[a]	Commitment US$ millions	Outcome	Bank performance	Borrower performance
East Asia and Pacific (continued)								
P004830	Vietnam I	R	Water Supply	1997–2005	99	Sat	Sat	Sat
P004833	Vietnam II	R	Urban Transport Improvement	1999–2006	43	M Sat	Sat	Unsat
P070197	Vietnam III	R	Urban Upgrading	2004–	222	—	—	—
P082295	Vietnam IV	R	Coastal Cities Environmental Sanitation	2007–	125	—	—	—
Europe and Central Asia								
P094225	Armenia	R	Third Social Investment Fund	2007–	25	—	—	—
P056192	Bosnia & Herzegovina I	W	Local Development	1999–2005	15	Sat	Sat	Sat
P070995	Bosnia & Herzegovina II	W	Community Development	2001–	15	—	—	—
P057950	Bosnia & Herzegovina III	R	Solid Waste Management	2002–	18	—	—	—
P083353	Bosnia & Herzegovina IV	W	Urban Infrastructure & Service	2005–	20	—	—	—
P065416	Croatia	W	Coastal Cities Pollution Control	2004–	48	—	—	—
P008417	Georgia I	w	Municipal Infrastructure Rehabilitation	1995–2000	18	M Unsat	M Unsat	M Unsat
P050910	Georgia II	W	Municipal Development & Decentralization	1998–2003	21	M Sat	M Sat	M Sat
P077368	Georgia III	W	Second Municipal Development & Decentralization	2003–	19	Sat	Sat	Sat
P008506	Kazakhstan I	R	Social Protection	1995–2002	41	Unsat	Sat	Unsat
P008500	Kazakhstan II	R	Atyrau Pilot Water	1999–2005	17	Sat	Sat	Sat
P079259	Kosovo	W	Second Community Development Fund	2004–07	4	M Sat	Sat	Sat
P050719	Kyrgyz Republic I	R	Urban Transport	2001–05	22	Sat	Sat	Sat
P083377	Kyrgyz Republic II	W	Small Towns Infrastructure & Capacity Building	2005–	15	—	—	—
P034584	Latvia	R	Municipal Services Development	1996–2002	27	M Sat	Sat	Sat
P035802	Lithuania	R	Municipal Development	1999–2005	20	Unsat	Unsat	Sat
P035082	Poland	W	Municipal Finance	1998–2002	22	Unsat	Unsat	Unsat
P042720	Russian Federation I	R	St. Petersburg Center City Rehabilitation	1997–2002	31	M Unsat	Unsat	Unsat
P064238	Russian Federation II	R	Northern Restructuring	2001–	80	—	—	—
P069063	Russian Federation III	R	St. Petersburg Economic Development	2003–	161	—	—	—
P082018	Russian Federation IV	R	Kazan Municipal Development	2005–07	125	H Sat	Sat	H Sat
P079027	Tajikistan	R	Municipal Infrastructure	2006–	15	—	—	—
P009065	Turkey I	R	Bursa Water & Sanitation	1993–2001	130	Sat	Sat	Sat
P081880	Turkey II	W	Municipal Services	2005–	275	—	—	—
P100383	Turkey III	R	Istanbul Municipal Infrastructure	2007–	322	—	—	—
P034083	Turkmenistan	R	Urban Transport	1997–2001	34	M Unsat	Unsat	Unsat
P095337	Ukraine	R	Urban Infrastructure	2008–	140	—	—	—
P049582	Uzbekistan	R	Tashkent Solid Waste Management	1998–2006	24	Sat	Sat	Sat

Latin America and the Caribbean

	ID	W/R	Project	Years	Amount				
Argentina I	P006060	W	Second Municipal Development	1995–2005	210	Sat	Sat	Sat	Sat
Argentina II	P060484	R	Basic Municipal Services	2006–	110	—	—	—	—
Argentina III	P070448	W	Subnational Govt. Public Sector Modernization	2006–	40	—	—	—	—
Belize	P006104	R	Belize City Infrastructure	1994–98	20	M Sat	Unsat	Unsat	Unsat
Bolivia I	P006190	W	Municipal Development	1994–2000	42	Sat	Sat	Sat	Sat
Bolivia II	P083979	R	Urban Infrastructure	2007–	30	—	—	—	—
Brazil I	P006524	W	Minas Municipal Development	1994–2002	150	Sat	Sat	Sat	Sat
Brazil II	P006436	W	Ceará Urban Development & Water Resource	1995–2004	140	M Sat	Sat	Sat	Sat
Brazil III	P006562	W	Bahia Municipal Infrast. Dev. & Mgmt.	1997–2005	100	Sat	Sat	Sat	Sat
Brazil IV	P081436	R	Bahia Poor Urban Areas Integrated Development	2006–	49	—	—	—	—
Brazil V	P089013	R	Municipal APL: Recife	2008–	33	—	—	—	—
Chile I	P006677	W	Municipal Development	1994–98	10	Sat	Sat	Sat	Sat
Chile II	P055480	W	Second Municipal Development	1999–2005	10	M Sat	M Sat	M Sat	M Sat
Colombia I	P006852	W	Municipal Development	1991–2001	60	Sat	Sat	Sat	Sat
Colombia II	P006872	R	Bogota Urban Transport	1996–2001	65	H Sat	H Sat	H Sat	H Sat
Colombia III	P039291	R	Urban Environment (TAL)	1996–2003	20	Sat	Sat	Sat	Sat
Colombia IV	P006861	W	Urban Infrastructure Services Development	1998–2004	75	Sat	Sat	Sat	Sat
Colombia V	P074726	R	Bogota Urban Services Project	2003–	100	—	—	—	—
Colombia VI	P082466	R	Integrated Mass Transit Systems	2004–	250	—	—	—	—
Colombia VII	P085727	R	Disaster Vulnerability Reduction Project (APL 2)	2006–	80	—	—	—	—
Ecuador I	P007123	W	First Municipal Development	1991–99	104	Sat	Sat	Sat	Sat
Ecuador II	P007128	R	Environmental Management	1996–2002	15	M Unsat	M Sat	Unsat	Unsat
Haiti	P007292	R	Port-Au-Prince Water Supply	1989–99	20	Unsat	Unsat	Unsat	Unsat
Honduras I	P064913	W	Natural Disaster Mitigation	2000–	11	—	—	—	—
Honduras II	P057859	R	Sustainable Coastal Tourism Project	2002–06	5	M Sat	M Sat	Sat	Sat
Honduras III	P088319	W	Barrio Ciudad	2006–	15	—	—	—	—
Honduras IV	P103881	R	Water & Sanitation Program	2007–	30	—	—	—	—
Mexico I	P007710	R	Northern Border Environment	1994–2004	368	M Unsat	M Unsat	Unsat	Unsat
Mexico II	P007612	R	Solid Waste	1994–2001	200	M Unsat	Unsat	Unsat	Unsat
Nicaragua	P064916	W	Natural Disaster Vulnerability Reduction	2001–	14	—	—	—	—

(Continues on the next page.)

Project ID	MDP	Type	Project name	Period[a]	Commitment US$ millions	Outcome	Bank performance	Borrower performance
Latin America and the Caribbean (continued)								
P035740	Peru I	R	Lima Transport	2004–	45	—	—	—
P082625	Peru II	R	Vilcanota Valley Rehabilitation & Management	2005–	5	—	—	—
P078894	Peru III	W	Second Real Property Rights	2006–	25	—	—	—
P008212	Venezuela I	W	Low-Income Barrios Improvement	1992–99	40	Sat	H Sat	Sat
P008210	Venezuela II	W	Urban Transport	1994–2002	100	Sat	Sat	Sat
P040174	Venezuela III	R	Caracas Slum Upgrading	1999–2006	61	M Sat	M Sat	M Sat
Middle East and North Africa								
P094229	Egypt, Arab Rep. of	R	Alexandria Development	2008–	100	—	—	—
P073433	Iran, Islamic Rep. of	R	Urban Upgrading & Housing Reform	2004–	80	—	—	—
P070958	Jordan I	W	Regional & Local Development	2007–	20	—	—	—
P081823	Jordan II	R	Cultural Heritage, Tourism & Urban Development	2007–	56	—	—	—
P050544	Lebanon I	W	First Municipal Infrastructure	2000–	80	—	—	—
P050529	Lebanon II	R	Cultural Heritage & Urban Development	2003–	32	—	—	—
P005524	Morocco	R	Fes Medina Rehabilitation	1999–2006	14	Unsat	Unsat	Unsat
P005687	Tunisia I	W	Municipal Sector Investment	1993–99	75	Sat	Sat	Sat
P046832	Tunisia II	W	Second Municipal Development	1997–2003	80	M Sat	Unsat	Sat
P064082	Tunisia III	R	Transport Sector Investment	2001–	38	—	—	—
P074398	Tunisia IV	W	Third Municipal Development	2003–	78	—	—	—
P043339	West Bank & Gaza I	R	Municipal Development	1996–2003	40	Unsat	Sat	Sat
P053985	West Bank & Gaza II	R	Bethlehem 2000	1999–2004	25	M Unsat	Sat	Sat
P058683	West Bank & Gaza III	R	Second Municipal Infrastructure Development	2000–05	14	Sat	Sat	Sat
P078212	West Bank & Gaza IV	W	Emergency Municipal Services Rehabilitation	2003–06	20	M Sat	Sat	M Sat
P005907	Yemen, Republic of I	R	Sana'a Water Supply & Sanitation	1999–2003	25	M Sat	Unsat	Sat
P070092	Yemen, Republic of II	R	Taiz Municipal Development & Flood Protection	2002–	45	—	—	—
P065111	Yemen, Republic of III	R	Port Cities Development Program	2003–	23	—	—	—
South Asia								
P083919	Afghanistan	R	Kabul Urban Reconstruction	2005–	25	—	—	—
P009467	Bangladesh I	R	Urban Development	1988–98	48	Unsat	Unsat	Unsat
P041887	Bangladesh II	W	Municipal Services	1999–	139	—	—	—
P057570	Bhutan	R	Urban Development	2000–06	11	M Unsat	M Sat	M Sat
P009872	India I	W	Tamil Nadu Urban Development	1988–98	300	M Sat	Sat	Sat

P050637	India II	W	Tamil Nadu Second Urban Development	1999–2005	105	Sat	Sat	Sat
P083780	India III	R	Third Tamil Nadu Urban Development	2006–	300	—	—	—
P079675	India IV	R	Karnataka Municipal Reform	2006–	216	—	—	—
P010305	Pakistan I	R	Punjab Urban Development	1988–98	90	M Sat	Sat	Sat
P010478	Pakistan II	R	North West Frontier Province Community Infrastructure	1996–2003	22	M Unsat	Unsat	Unsat
P083929	Pakistan III	W	Punjab Municipal Services Improvement	2006–	50	—	—	—
P010467	Sri Lanka	R	Colombo Environment Improvement	1995–2001	39	Unsat	Unsat	Unsat

Source: World Bank data.

Note: MDP = municipal development project; R = retail; W = wholesale; — = not rated, as project not closed yet. **Ratings:** H Sat = highly satisfactory; M Sat = moderately satisfactory; Sat = satisfactory; M Unsat = moderately unsatisfactory; Unsat = unsatisfactory; H Unsat = highly unsatisfactory.

a. Entry amd exit years; projects not yet closed just show entry year.

APPENDIX B: BANKING ON MUNICIPALITIES: WORLD BANK SUPPORT IN SUB-SAHARAN AFRICA

Bank Support

With 280 million people—36 percent of the total population—living in cities, the Sub-Saharan Africa Region is experiencing rapid urban population growth of 3.9 percent per annum. The World Bank financed 52 municipal development projects (MDPs) in this Region that were active during 1998–2008, with loan commitments of $2.4 billion. The portfolio aimed to strengthen the management of 656 municipalities in 27 countries.

By the number of MDPs, the most active borrowers were Uganda (5 projects), Ethiopia (4), Ghana (4), Madagascar (3), Benin (3), and Mozambique (3). The following countries hosted two MDPs each: Burkina Faso, Guinea, Mali, Mauritania, Niger, Nigeria, Senegal, Swaziland, and Tanzania. Another 12 countries had just 1 each: Burundi, Cameroon, Chad, Côte d'Ivoire, The Gambia, Kenya, Malawi, Rwanda, South Africa, Togo, Zambia, and Zimbabwe. Nearly all the MDPs—more than 90 percent of the total—were thus implemented in low-income countries. The MDP portfolio covered all countries in the Region with large urban populations (15 million plus) except for the Democratic Republic of Congo and Sudan.

Portfolio Performance

With 75 percent of projects achieving satisfactory outcomes, the Region's MDP performance was similar to that of the worldwide portfolio. In terms of Bank performance, Sub-Saharan Africa's MDPs did better, with 81 percent satisfactory, against a Bank-wide average of 78 percent satisfactory. For borrower performance, the Region lagged behind, with 69 percent satisfactory against 75 percent satisfactory Bank-wide.

Table B.1: Summary of MDP Portfolio, 1998–2008

Completed (number)	32
Completed MDPs (% satisfactory)	75
Ongoing MDPs (number)	20
IBRD commitments (US$ million)	174
IDA commitments (US$ million)	2,179
Bank commitments per completed MDP (US$ million)	42
Commitments per ongoing MDP (US$ million)	56
Wholesale MDPs (number)	12
Retail MDPs (number)	40
Countries served (number)	27
Municipalities served (number)	656

Source: World Bank data.
Note: IBRD = International Bank for Reconstruction and Development; IDA = International Development Association; MDP = municipal development project.

Of particular note were two MDPs that achieved highly satisfactory outcomes. These can serve as model operations for others to emulate.

The first, **Benin I,** helped improve urban services in the country's two largest cities, Cotonou (population 690,584) and Porto Novo (population 234,168). This result was confirmed by beneficiary assessments at completion and was helped by the introduction of delegated contract management practices. These enabled rapid processing and execution of service contracts with local small and medium-size enterprises that provided higher-quality, lower-cost urban infrastructure services and left municipal administrations more time to concentrate on their planning and programming tasks.

The second highly satisfactory MDP, **Senegal I,** was a wholesale operation that helped 67 municipalities throughout the country strengthen their

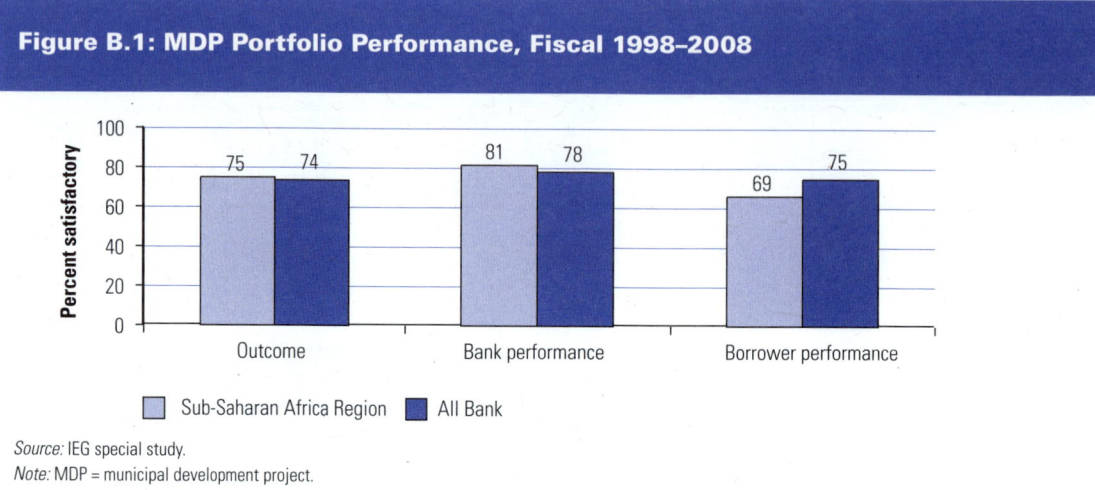

Figure B.1: MDP Portfolio Performance, Fiscal 1998–2008

Source: IEG special study.

Note: MDP = municipal development project.

financial and organizational management and improve programming of investments in urban infrastructure and services. The project achieved this through what were called "municipal contracts," participating agreements between central and individual local governments with benchmarks for municipal reform. Currently, more than 170 municipalities across French-speaking West Africa are implementing such contracts. The short-term results of the reforms were an increased municipal capacity to invest. Over 2001–03, for instance, municipal capital investment as a share of current revenues rose from 10 to 17 percent.

Other operations with good outcomes in Sub-Saharan Africa included all five MDPs in Uganda. **Uganda I** introduced private sector participation in the municipal services of the capital Kampala (population 1.4 million). Flooding in that city was curbed thanks to **Uganda II's** rehabilitation of the Nakivubo Channel. In providing investment funds and technical assistance to other municipalities, **Uganda III** strengthened municipal management across the country, using a wholesale approach. **Uganda IV** consolidated this approach by helping 30 municipalities tighten their management controls, deploying novel distance learning techniques to this end.

Ghana also had a string of successful MDPs. **Ghana I** brought significant service improvements, notably solid waste and stronger manage-

ment, to six municipalities. This success was extended to 11 more municipalities by **Ghana II. Ghana IV** took the wholesale model further by investing intensely in financial and technical training for the staff of 23 municipalities through the national Institute of Local Government Studies, which itself came out of the project considerably strengthened.

Madagascar II and **III** helped municipalities improve municipal services through local agreements with an AGETIP-style provider. By investing in sewerage and solid waste in particular, **Tanzania I** improved environmental management in eight municipalities that a later government assessment found be the best in the country. Initially conceived as a retail operation only for Niamey (population 774,237) and Dogondoutchi (population 31,767), **Niger I** was successfully broadened as a wholesale operation that, among other things, introduced new digital cartography skills into urban planning in 19 other municipalities.

Some MDPs performed poorly, however. **Côte D'Ivoire's MDP** delivered fewer than half the service improvements planned as the country situation became more volatile and central government support for the operation waned. **Ethiopia I** failed to address the major issues of budgeting, accounting, and financial management of the client municipality of Addis Ababa (population 2.8 million), and infrastructure investments for which demand was weak yielded inadequate returns. **Nigeria I** failed to build municipal management capabilities in Oyo State as intended, because of unresolved conflicts among the parties that led to implementation delays and cancellation of key components. **Mozambique I** did not implement the majority of the project's physical components because of procurement problems, inadequate Bank-borrower communication, and poor performance by consultants.

Better City Planning

More information

Particularly notable have been MDP efforts and results of obtaining better information about spatial configuration of cities. **Burkina Faso I,** for instance, helped create an information system and database for urban management based on street address mapping in the municipalities of Ougadougou (population 1.1 million) and Bobo Dioulasso (population 360,106). **Niger I** introduced a set of simple planning and programming tools covering digital cartography and the production of an atlas, initially for 2 cities but extended through a wholesale approach to 21 cities in all. Under **Ghana II,** maps were produced for 11 municipalities, leading to property valuations for twice as many properties as planned; only two municipalities ultimately developed land use structure plans on this basis.

Monitoring and evaluation

Swaziland I incorporated a good monitoring and evaluation (M&E) framework with clearly designed performance indicators that enabled a clear comparison of targeted and actual results, as well as of how far the municipalities had come from the baseline. **Mali I** also had good M&E, although its baseline references were less clear. **Uganda III** improved the evaluative capacity of the Ministry of Local Government, and **Uganda IV** helped the project implementation unit consolidate project-specific information that made it possible to undertake an evaluation of project outcomes.

Mozambique II and **Burkina Faso I** provided results frameworks with specific outputs and outcomes, but the latter were not always measurable, and baseline information was generally

Table B.2: Municipal Management Focus of Region Portfolio

Share of all MDPs with a project design focus on:	Completed	Ongoing
City planning		
In objectives (%)	28	15
In components (%)	44	55
Municipal finance		
In objectives (%)	75	35
In components (%)	56	90
Service delivery		
In objectives (%)	94	85
In components (%)	97	95
Number of all MDPs	32	20

Source: IEG special study.

Note: MDP = municipal development project.

missing. M&E systems of several MDPs were weakened by a focus on project outputs; this and other factors resulted in the inadequate performance of the operations. IEG found this to be case for **Guinea I,** the **Kenya MDP, Tanzania I,** and the **Togo MDP.**

Urban and spatial planning

Several MDPs made important contributions to the urban planning capabilities of client municipalities. Under guidance and technical assistance through **Mali I,** five municipalities prepared strategic long-term physical and spatial plans that particularly helped them better understand the workings of the land markets in their cities. Through a wholesale approach, **Mauritania I** introduced several management instruments, including urban plans, inventories of assets, and priority investment plans that were widely accepted by the local elected officials and staff of 13 municipalities.

Through **Uganda II** and **III,** the municipality of Kampala (population 1.4 million) prepared its Drainage Master Plan and Urban Transport Improvement Strategy. Moving toward the wholesale model of MDP, **Uganda IV** helped 30 municipalities make their existing municipal planning committees more functional, resulting in 90 percent of them preparing 3-year development plans. In **Benin I,** in addition to the successful project efforts to strengthen urban planning at the municipal level, the central government itself adopted a declaration of urban policy, through which it elaborated a coherent long-term strategy for urban planning, including its environmental and sanitary aspects.

Investment planning and strategies

MDP results were thin in a Region where development projects often propose ad hoc planning and implementation arrangements beyond the formal framework of central and local government. Thus, under **Mozambique I,** the five client municipalities that had prepared urban land-use and structure plans saw none of them result in the intended municipal investment strategies.

Stronger Municipal Finances

Better financial management

There is considerable evidence of MDP technical assistance and support helping municipalities improve their financial reporting and management. Under **Mali I,** for instance, three of the project's five targeted municipalities set up computerized accounting. More would have been achieved had there not been a shortage of municipal staff qualified in finance and programming. This points to the need for more basic training in municipal financial management in the future.

Uganda I and **II** enhanced the Kampala municipality's ability to plan, manage, and execute complex investment decisions and report on them, but roles and responsibilities for executing them remained ill defined at the project's end. This retail MDP focused on one municipality that was particularly prone to political interference in day-to-day operations. **Uganda III** and **IV,** in contrast, helped a much larger number of municipalities strengthen and harmonize their planning and budgeting processes. The project-created Audit Compliance Unit in the central government provided a strong incentive for municipalities to bring their financial records up to date and make them audit compliant.

Under **Senegal I,** a wholesale operation aimed at 67 municipalities throughout the country,

project audits confirmed that municipal financial budgeting was placed on a sound footing in all of them for the first time. This MDP also prepared the municipalities for incurring debt and managing debt service. In actual practice, their financial management was solid, as reflected in their being up to date in 95 percent of their loan repayments. **Tanzania I** and **Zimbabwe's MDP** helped the targeted municipalities—10 and 21, respectively—routinely prepare and deliver up-to-date and audited accounts.

Mobilizing own revenues

Evidence is beginning to emerge that municipalities assisted by MDP operations strengthened their revenue mobilization, perhaps more so than unassisted municipalities, although robust evidence of control group performance remains thin. Thus, under **Uganda III** and **IV,** some 30 municipalities saw own revenues increase by 40 percent in real terms, mainly because of computer processing of financial reports that highlighted arrears and areas of lax tax effort more promptly. Under **Swaziland I,** the 4 client municipalities extended property tax collection from 65 to 80 percent of eligible properties following training of tax collectors, supervisors, and billing and finance staff. **Tanzania I** enabled municipalities to more than double their own revenues, though from a low base, over the project period with the help of modern computer mapping and accounting. The **Togo MDP** introduced improved collection procedures and penalties for nonpayment, a computerized tax registry, and transparent methods for assessing property values, but the impact of all these measures on revenue collection is not known. Technical assistance through **Benin II** enabled its three municipal clients to exceed targeted own-revenue growth. **Burkina Faso I** saw revenue collection nearly double in the country's two largest municipalities after they developed a residential tax database with the help of project technical assistance.

In contrast, elections dampened the political will to pursue energetic local tax collection in Kampala under **Uganda I** and **II.** Similar constraints prevented the five client municipalities of **Mali I** from actually collecting revenues through a new urban tax that had been formally instituted but not acted on, leaving the municipal finances of Bamako (population 1.3 million) and Mopti (population 108,456) in deficit.

Aside from taxation itself, the municipality of Lomé (population 718,797) was able to create a new municipal agency with the help of the **Togo MDP;** this agency managed thriving local markets and collected user fees. Similar user charges enhanced the revenues of six municipalities under **Ghana I.** Progress with revenue mobilization continued among municipalities participating in **Ghana II** and **III** but slowed somewhat in the face of municipal resistance to setting user charges high enough to cover costs. Revenue performance was weak under **Nigeria I** and left municipal billing and collection machinery at the local level weak. Though **Ethiopia I** did adopt cost recovery for housing and some municipal services, it made them less affordable to the poor in the short run.

Municipal creditworthiness and debt management

To date, MDPs have done little to involve municipalities in local credit markets, although more can be expected in the future as incipient markets develop.

Private finance participation

Only modest results have been reported. **Swaziland MDP's** attempts to bring together local governments and private sector financial institutions did lead to some private financing of municipal services on a small scale in the capital Mbabane (population 76, 218). Under **Mauritania I,** better municipal management gave more confidence for private suppliers to work with the 13 MDP municipalities in that country.

Improved Service Provision

Investment priorities

Of 32 completed operations, more than half reported economic rates of return (ERRs) at both appraisal and completion, the highest proportion for any Region. ERR estimates at completion ranged from 7 to 84 percent, exceeding appraisal

ERRs in half the cases. Estimates of internal rates of return were more readily available for road- and water-related components. The main issues relating to ERRs were partial coverage of the investment, lack of credible data, and, still in a few cases, an apparent lack of appreciation for the importance of conducting an economic cost-benefit analysis.

Ghana I reported the highest ERR of 82 percent after detailed assessments showed the high impact of below-cost road improvements in the municipality of Accra (population 2.0 million) that accounted for one-third of the MDP project costs. Efficient upgrading of existing urban roads in 11 other municipalities also explained the 68 percent ERR reported for **Ghana II,** although in this case the estimate covered only 13 percent of the total project costs.

Seven more successful MDPs reported high ERRs in the 25–40 percent range. **Benin II** also yielded a 73 percent ERR, nearly five times the appraisal estimate, owing to much higher traffic volumes than expected on the urban road improvements that accounted for most of the project costs. **The Gambia MDP** reported a 38 percent ERR for road paving and drainage works in two municipalities; again, these components accounted for only about one-fifth of the total project cost. **Burkina Faso I** yielded a 33 percent ERR, thanks to the rehabilitation of urban roads and streets in the country's two main cities, components that accounted for 40 percent of project costs.

Interestingly, **Niger I** found ERRs in the 20–41 percent range for other components, such as bus stations, slaughterhouses, public latrines, and leisure parks, using a beneficiary willingness-to-pay concept. A good cost-benefit analysis through **Uganda II** that carefully identified the counterfactual and the flood-protection benefits to the municipality of Kampala of reducing building and infrastructure damage and of time savings yielded a 25 percent ERR at completion. **Tanzania I** also yielded an ERR of 25 percent, based on the benefits of road and water supply improvements across 10 municipalities, accounting for 55 percent of project costs.

Even though the Region has done the most cost-benefit analysis of all Regions, several MDPs did not include ERR estimates at completion even of municipal infrastructure and service provision components that are amenable to cost-benefit analysis. Lack of adequate data was most commonly given as the reason for not estimating ERR.

Procurement

Municipalities' experience in taking charge of procurement has been mixed, but there has been progress. Implementation of **Mozambique I** was stalled by municipalities' difficulties in meeting procurement norms. In contrast, more recently **Tanzania I** gave 10 municipalities the opportunity to manage procurement effectively for the first time.

Operations and maintenance

IEG found municipal clients of MDPs were beginning to give more attention to operations and maintenance (O&M). Under the **Kenya MDP,** for instance, four municipalities did more O&M because of the incentive of special funding provided by the National Road Fund. Nearly all municipal water utilities funded O&M from their own budgets under **Tanzania I** for the first time. Although **Uganda II** and **III** raised the profile of O&M in the eyes of municipalities in Kampala, the municipality was not able to raise all the revenue needed to sustain this over the long run. The sustained impact of improved municipal services under **Benin I** and **II** is only ensured if the three client municipalities continue to mobilize the necessary revenues on their own. However, municipal O&M continues to be weak in many municipalities, as the results of the **Côte d'Ivoire MDP, Swaziland I,** and the **Zambia MDP** showed.

Services—Most affected sectors

MDPs provided a wide range of municipal services, from low-income area upgrading; to urban road and street paving and drainage works; to water and basic sanitation, other environmental improvements, and urban transport. In upgrading existing low-income areas, **Burkina Faso I** was particularly effective, using beneficiary participation. Under **Benin I**

and **II,** drainage works helped protect 403,000 people in 6 municipalities against flooding. **Ghana I** and **IV** had an impact on 11 municipalities by rehabilitating urban roads and markets while increasing opportunities for small businesses in vehicle repair and commerce.

Senegal I financed 421 basic infrastructure subprojects across Senegal's 67 urban municipalities and introduced systematic street address systems for the first time in 11 of them. The **Zimbabwe MDP** enabled 21 municipalities to rehabilitate urban roads and extend water supply and basic sanitation. Similar improvements to basic sanitation under **Guinea I** and **Mali I** may have contributed to a steep decline in deaths from cholera. Water metering and network improvements enabled **Swaziland I** to reduce unaccounted-for water in four municipalities. Sewage treatment under **Tanzania I** meant that the effluent quality nearly met World Health Organization standards in three municipalities. Urban transport was less of an MDP focus in Africa than in other Regions, but indirectly **Uganda II** brought considerable improvements to traffic flows in Kampala by mitigating the impact of regular flooding prior to the completion of the Nakivubo channel.

Services—Private provision

MDPs made considerable efforts to engage private operators in the provision of municipal service in several countries. Some results were achieved, but there is still a long way to go. Under **Uganda I** and **III,** for instance, the fact that nearly all the infrastructure investment was privately contracted was itself a significant result for the municipality of Kampala, which had traditionally done its own work. The use of force account also ceased following **Madagascar II** and the **Zambia MDP. Ghana I** and **Senegal I** strengthened contractor and consulting industries within their respective countries.

The competitive private sector approach to municipal service investment received a boost under **Tanzania I.** That project, as well as **Burkina Faso I, Ghana III,** and **Guinea I,** provided openings for private solid waste collec-

Box B.1: Key to MDPs Referred to in Text

Benin: I—Urban Rehabilitation & Management; II—First Decentralized City Management; III—Second Decentralized City Management. **Burkina Faso:** I—Urban Environment; II—Decentralized Urban Capacity Building. **Burundi:** Public Works & Employment Creation. **Cameroon:** Urban & Water Development Support. **Chad:** Urban Development. **Côte d'Ivoire:** Municipal Support. **Ethiopia:** I—Second Addis Urban Development; II—Capacity Building for Decentralized Service Delivery; III—Public Sector Capacity Building; IV—Urban Water Supply & Sanitation. **The Gambia:** Poverty Alleviation & Capacity Building. **Ghana:** I—Second Urban Development; II—Local Government Development; III—Urban Environment & Sanitation; IV—Fifth Urban Development. **Guinea:** I—Third Urban Development (APL); II—Third Urban Development (Phase 2). **Kenya:** Urban Transport. **Madagascar:** I—Antananarivo Plain Development; II—Antananarivo Urban Works Pilot; III—Urban Infrastructure. **Malawi:** Local Government Development. **Mali:** I—Urban Development & Decentralization; II—Second Transport Sector.

Mauritania: I—Urban Infrastructure & Pilot Decentralization; II—Urban Development Program. **Mozambique:** I—Local Government Reform & Engineering; II—Municipal Development; III—Maputo Municipal Development Program. **Niger:** I—Urban Infrastructure Rehabilitation; II—Local Urban Infrastructure Development. **Nigeria:** I—Oyo State Urban Development; II—Lagos Metropolitan Development & Governance. **Rwanda:** Urban Infrastructure & City Management. **Senegal:** I—Urban Development & Decentralization Program; II—Local Authorities Development Program. **South Africa:** Municipal Financial Management. **Swaziland:** I—Urban Development; II—Local Government. **Tanzania:** I—Urban Sector Rehabilitation; II—Local Government Support. **Togo:** Lomé Urban Development. **Uganda:** I—First Urban Development; II—Nakivubo Channel Rehabilitation; III—Local Government Development Program; IV—Economic & Financial Management; V—Kampala Institutional & Infrastructure Development. **Zambia:** Urban Restructuring. **Zimbabwe:** Urban Sector & Regional Development.

Source: IEG.

tion operators, but a shortage of qualified local labor was a major constraint in sustaining these services. Urban road and street maintenance contracts under these projects attracted more private sector bids.

Income level of beneficiaries—Poverty reduction

Altogether, 60 percent of MDPs have objectives explicitly focused on the poor and on poverty reduction. Some MDP results were quite impressive. **Benin I, Madagascar III, Niger I,** and **The Gambia** and **Togo MDPs** generated jobs for the poor. These jobs came through project construction and required more than 1.3 million person-days of labor-intensive employment, usually through local small and medium-sized enterprises contracted for road and drainage maintenance and other works.

Municipal services provided through **Burkina Faso I, Ghana I, Mali I, Mauritania I, Niger I, Nigeria I,** and **Tanzania I** all served low-income and squatter settlements through infrastructure and water and sanitation, health facilities, access roads, public lighting, school fencing, and green

spaces efforts. Under **Ghana III,** in all project cities, lower-income communities benefited: the estimated number of beneficiaries for household latrines was 60,000, for school latrines 100,000, and for public latrines 30,000. In most cases, road construction and rehabilitation opened access between the poor neighborhoods and the economic centers of the cities and improved scope for informal and small-scale income-generating activities.

Conclusions

- Across Regions, MDPs in Sub-Saharan Africa have kept the greatest focus on improving the lives of the poor.
- Increasing the number of wholesale MDPs would be constrained in a Region with few higher-level agencies that are ready to take on the intermediation function that such operations require.
- Across countries, MDP performance with M&E varies considerably, pointing to opportunities for fruitful exchanges of experiences. Their performance in the use of cost-benefit analysis has been relatively good, pointing to opportunities to apply the techniques in other Regions.

APPENDIX C: BANKING ON MUNICIPALITIES:
WORLD BANK SUPPORT IN EAST ASIA AND PACIFIC

Bank Support

East Asia and Pacific has the largest urban population of any Bank Region; 805 million people—42 percent of the total population—live in cities, and urbanization continues at a rapid pace, with the population in cities growing by 2.9 percent annually. The World Bank, through 44 MDPs active during the 1998–2008 decade, committed $5.7 billion to urban development. This portfolio aimed to strengthen the management of 445 municipalities across 16 countries. By number of MDPs, the most active borrowers were China (23 projects) and Indonesia (12), followed by a newer MDP borrower, Vietnam (4), and an older one, the Philippines (3). In addition, Mongolia and Korea hosted 1 MDP each. Thus, nearly all of the Region's MDPs, 86 percent, were in lower-middle-income countries. Countries in this Region with large urban populations (15 million plus) but no Bank-financed MDPs are Thailand and Myanmar.

Portfolio Performance

On average, MDPs in the Region are strong performers, with 80 percent achieving satisfactory outcomes. Also, 90 percent had satisfactory Bank performance, and 83 percent had satisfactory borrower performance, all well above averages for the worldwide MDP portfolio.

Although no project had an outcome rating of highly satisfactory, there are numerous examples of successful MDPs in several countries in this Region that can serve as models for MDPs elsewhere. **China III,** thanks to an outstanding municipal team in the megacity of Tianjin (population 10.3 million), succeeded on several fronts, building and operating a solid waste sanitary disposal facility that became a model for

Table C.1: Summary of MDP Portfolio, 1998–2008	
Completed (number)	30
Completed MDPs (% satisfactory)	80
Ongoing MDPs (number)	14
IBRD commitments (US$ million)	4,512
IDA commitments (US$ million)	1,158
Bank commitments per completed MDP (US$ million)	126
Commitments per ongoing MDP (US$ million)	136
Wholesale MDPs (number)	11
Retail MDPs (number)	33
Countries served (number)	6
Municipalities served (number)	445

Source: World Bank data.
Note: IBRD = International Bank for Reconstruction and Development; IDA = International Development Association; MDP = municipal development project.

China, increasing sewage collection and treatment, improving traffic management, and consolidating municipal planning capability. **Philippines I** was particularly successful at upgrading low-income areas by developing new local markets and in training 9,129 staff from 74 municipalities. These efforts resulted in a new municipal management style that was better adapted to the increasing responsibilities under decentralization. **China IV** got good results across the board in Zhejiang Province by improving municipal management as it related to urban planning, land development, and environment in key cities that offered among the best investment climates in China. **Indonesia V** produced good results in five municipalities in Kalimantan, particularly through the successful Kampung Improvement Program in Pontianak (population 455,173).

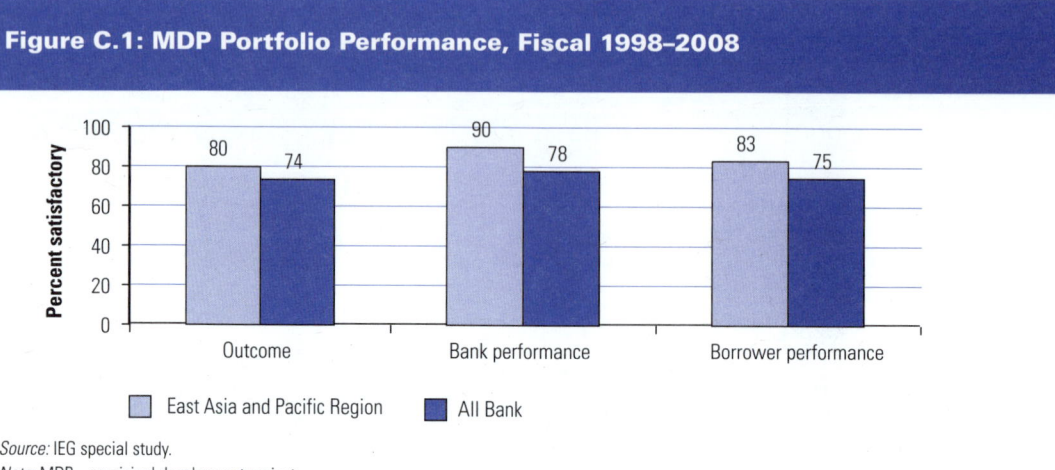

Figure C.1: MDP Portfolio Performance, Fiscal 1998–2008

Source: IEG special study.

Note: MDP = municipal development project.

Under **Indonesia XIX,** which focused on municipal innovations, the municipality of Bogor (population 769,000) was particularly successful in developing a lively and informative public Web site that was an online version of the earlier public information booths. There were significant environmental gains in improved water supply and sewage and solid waste disposal through **China VII** and **VIII** in Shanghai and Liaoning, respectively. Directly focused on retooling municipal management, **China IX** was effective in helping four municipalities manage the deep structural reform involving the divesti-

ture of enterprise housing. The **Mongolia MDP** helped develop the country's capability to design, build, and operate urban services through the successful improvements the project brought to the water supply of the municipality of Ulaanbataar (population 844,818).

Some MDPs in the Region performed poorly. **Indonesia III** achieved little, as the repeated turnover in municipal leadership in Surabaya (population 2.4 million) undermined commitment to agreements. This led to inaction on service provision to the city that should have called for a thorough project reappraisal. **China XI** did not lead to the hoped-for reduction of air pollution by replacing old industrial plants in the municipality of Chongqing (population 32 million) because of the slow divestiture of such plants and the cancellation of the project's credit component. Pollution did decline, but not because of the project; instead, that improvement occurred because of the slow-down of industrial activity.

Indonesia VII intended to improve solid waste and sewage treatment services in 41 municipalities in Sulawesi, but it was only partly implemented because of lack of government commitment and concerns over misuse of funds. This left municipalities without the management progress intended, especially in operations and

Table C.2: Municipal Management Focus of Region Portfolio

Share of all MDPs with a project design focus on:	Completed	Ongoing
City planning		
In objectives (%)	50	50
In components (%)	40	64
Municipal finance		
In objectives (%)	60	21
In components (%)	33	64
Service delivery		
In objectives (%)	90	100
In components (%)	97	93
Number of all MDPs	30	14

Source: IEG special study.

Note: MDP = municipal development project.

maintenance (O&M), the project's model of which was too complicated to administer.

Better City Planning

More information

Some MDPs in the Region improved the information available to municipalities. Under **China III,** for instance, the municipality of Tianjin (population 10.3 million) was able to develop a real-time information system for the megacity's intense traffic. Under **Indonesia IX,** Bogor's success in assembling and disseminating information on municipal services publicly on the Web is an important information system achievement.

Monitoring & evaluation

M&E systems exhibit the weaknesses found in other Regions and sectors. Thus, under **China IV** in Zhejiang Province, an operation that excelled in many other respects, M&E did little more than count and cost the delivery of individual subprojects. **China XII,** in Yunnan Province, did a little better with monitoring the project's physical achievements, but it fell short on verifying progress on the institutional front. M&E for **Indonesia II** and **VI** ventured little beyond counting the number of subproject contracts awarded and the amount of disbursements. This meant that M&E was able to provide precise information about the number of community toilets built and their exact unit costs, but not how much those facilities were used—which proved to be very little. The Independent Evaluation Group (IEG) saw communal toilet blocks designed for 15 families being used by only 1 or 2.

China X in Hubei had weak M&E, as the indicators were defined too broadly to be measurable. The M&E of **China IX** suffered the classic shortcoming of not providing baseline values for 38 indicators that were selected to measure progress in divesting state-owned enterprise housing.

Even when indicators are good, M&E problems can arise. This happened when measuring water quality of the environmentally stressed Huangpo River in Shanghai under **China VII.** Data on baseline and endline water quality were available, but the samples were drawn from different locations on the river. Furthermore, the monitoring station built under the project was not fully operational. An implementation weakness undermined the effectiveness of M&E for **China XV** in Sichuan Province, where records of measurement of the well-designed performance indicators were not systematically kept.

But even when its design is weak, M&E can be improved during implementation, as when the strong local team of **China III** in Tianjin, at its own initiative, incorporated outcome indicators to measure greater municipal management effectiveness, which had been overlooked by the initial M&E design. Finally, one of the most complete M&E systems was introduced through **Vietnam I,** where four project municipalities used indicators that that covered all aspects of improvement in water supply service, ranging from physical provision to management efficiency.

Urban and spatial planning

MDPs have achieved a lot, especially in China, where many local municipalities have embraced city planning in recent years. Thus, under **China I,** the Urban Master Plan of Beijing (population 14.9 million) incorporated for the first time environmental priorities of the municipal environmental protection bureau. **China III** helped Tianjin prepare its Master Plan and consolidate it with the indicative budget for 2005–20, again for the first time. Particularly for the city of Ningbo in Zhejiang Province, **China IV** strengthened its long-term land use planning through technical assistance and firmly embedded the conservation of historic and cultural monuments into its city center planning, now recognized as one of China's best.

On the urban transport side, two operations, **China II** and **VI,** enabled Shanghai (population 14.6 million) to improve its transport planning by providing expert input. Other countries also saw some of their city planning improve through MDP assistance. Thus, under **Indonesia X,** nine municipalities prepared local environmental plans and strategies for the first time, one of which was the critical Drainage Master Plan for Jakarta (population 8.5 million). Through **Philippines I,** some 70 municipalities learned how to incorporate specific investments of the operation in subprojects into their local city plans.

More innovative approaches to planning did not always succeed. Under **Indonesia II** support for Integrated Urban Infrastructure Development Planning, a modernized and multisectoral approach to planning, made only modest inroads in smaller municipalities, which found it too complex and were more comfortable with the traditional sectoral approach they knew well.

Investment planning and strategies

MDPs in the Region generally did not require client municipalities to strengthen the management of their investment planning and strategies. Larger municipalities in particular often had their own investment plans in place before the MDP.

Stronger Municipal Finances

Better financial management

In China, a number of municipalities improved their financial management and accounting procedures with the help of MDPs. **China III,** for instance, helped the mega-municipality of Tianjin integrate different financial networks across its very large organization, where computerization of all accounts within a local area network has now become standard. **China V** helped improve cost recovery for water supply, allowing four municipalities in southern Jiangsu Province to cover operating, if not investment, costs. The municipal audit bureau of Shanghai (population 14.6 million) was quickly able to adopt international accounting standards, as required by **China VII.**

Mobilizing own revenues

Revenue enhancement through MDPs in the Region focused particularly on increasing direct cost recovery from the project investments themselves, rather than seeking broader improvements in general revenues. In practice, cost recovery has been as challenging in this Region as in others. **China VII** was unable to raise tariffs enough to enable five municipal sanitation companies in Liaoning Province to cover their operating costs. **China XII** did not enable the five municipal sanitation utilities in Yunnan Province to achieve full cost recovery, but there has been some progress in tariff adjustment. **China X** reported similar constraints in limiting cost recovery, but for solid waste management in Hubei Province.

Although the details are scarce, **Indonesia II** did report enhanced revenue collection among the 45 municipalities assisted by the project in East Java and Bali. Under **Indonesia IV,** however, inflation eroded effective cost recovery of municipal water utilities in Semarang (population 1.3 million) and Surakarta (population 555,308). **Mongolia's MDP** achieved a lot on the municipal finance front, but not the full financial autonomy for the municipal sanitation utility of Ulaanbataar (population 844,818) promised by the project's ambitious objectives. Nevertheless, computerized billing worked well and considerably enhanced tariff collections. **Philippines I** achieved significant results across the 74 client municipalities, especially through property tax cadastres that more than doubled assessed values; actual tax collections increased by 64 percent over the 1994–2001 project period. **Vietnam's MDP** enabled municipal water supply utilities in Hanoi (population 1.4 million) and Haiphong (population 602,695) to cover their O&M costs and even build up some reserves.

Municipal creditworthiness and debt management

This aspect of municipal management was explored on a small scale. **Philippines I's** Municipal Development Fund established a long-term credit window that loaned $34 million to eligible municipalities. Although the lending was small scale relative to municipal needs, the credit mechanism did introduce 74 municipalities across the country to debt service management.

Private finance participation

IEG found little evidence of significant effort by MDPs to enhance private finance for municipal services in the Region.

Improved Service Provision

Investment priorities

Some 60 percent of MDPs provided ERR estimates for project investments at appraisal and completion. They were widely used for MDPs completed in China. **China XIII** yielded a 39 percent ERR based on users' willingness to pay for sanitation services in 38 municipalities in Shandong Province. **China II** and **VII** reported ERRs of 28 percent, from the benefits of time and operating cost savings from improved traffic flows in Shanghai. **China III** led to ERRs of 23 percent Tianjin, based on benefits accruing principally from urban land development for housing and industrial uses.

But a more robust economic analysis, distinguishing new businesses from those that had simply transferred to the **China IV** project area in Shaoxing (population 421,283) in Zhejiang Province, would have evaluated the project's land development more precisely. Satisfactory ERRs in the 14–18 percent range were reported elsewhere through **Mongolia's** and **Vietnam's MDPs,** as well as **Indonesia II.** In some cases, unpersuasive reasons were given for project teams not estimating even simplified internal rates of return. Thus, excessive cost and time needed were cited as reasons for not estimating an ERR for **China VII,** despite the high cost of the project investment incurred to improve the quality of the water supply to Shanghai.

Procurement

MDPs in this Region reported few significant results, as far as changes in procurement practice at the municipal level are concerned. One exception was **China III,** through which the municipality of Tianjin conducted successful international competitive bidding to establish the Shuangkou solid waste disposal site, China's first fully sanitary landfill, complete with an onsite leachate treatment plant that became a model operation for the country.

Operations and maintenance

The results of some MDPs call for municipalities to pay more attention to assuring financing for ongoing operations of existing infrastructure and municipal services. For instance, a municipal water supply system provided under **Indonesia II** for the Kintamani district of Denpasar (population 405,923) in Bali fell into disuse, as the local authorities could not afford to pay to operate the necessary pumps for more than a fraction of the time needed. In Sulawesi, **Indonesia VII's** 41 client municipalities were unable to adopt the project's "performance-oriented maintenance management systems," which they found too complicated. In Western Java **Indonesia X** saw that continuing uncertainties about the funding mechanisms for municipal waste management corporations put the project's urban environmental achievements at risk. **China XV,** completed in 2007, reported that the four beneficiary municipalities needed to raise more revenues to ensure O&M funding.

Services—Most affected sectors

MDPs in this Region provided support to municipalities to improve services connected with water supply, basic sanitation, and other environmental improvements. In addition, they helped improve urban transport, through new urban roads, street paving, and drainage and traffic management measures. The upgrading of low-income areas through the introduction of basic infrastructure continues through MDPs in East Asia, but on a smaller scale than before, and elsewhere.

To improve the municipal management of water supply, MDPs made some notable achievements in China in particular. A significant environmental and public health gain for more than 8 million inhabitants of Shanghai was the result of **China VII's** provision of a safer water supply. This was done by implementing a major intake upriver in less-polluted reaches of the environmentally stressed Huangpo River, as well as implementing mitigation measures in solid waste collection and disposal and restricting use of agricultural fertilizers to prevent runoff from further polluting the river. Major municipal water treatment plants under **China IV** improved service quality to the people living in key cities of Zhejiang Province, Hangzhou (population 1.9 million), Ningbo (population 719,867), and Wenzhou (population 865,672).

MDPs also improved basic sanitation. The innovative, low-cost, small-scale "modular" approach to sewage treatment was adopted by the municipality of Malang (population 747,000) under **Indonesia VI.** However, its success was limited, as low-income residents continued to discharge sewage without charge into storm drains, rather than paying the (modest) fee imposed by the new system.

MDPs made more progress helping municipalities improve their solid waste management, especially in the final disposal of waste. **China III** led to the building and operation of the country's first sanitary landfill at Shuangkou near Tianjin—now considered a successful model nationwide. This experience built on earlier successful efforts to improve solid waste disposal in Beijing under **China I.** Under **China X,** the municipality of Xianfang (population 462,956) in Hubei Province succeeded in disposing of 100 percent of its collected solid waste in a sanitary landfill built by the project. **Indonesia V** introduced controlled landfills to five municipalities in Kalimantan that also closed down their earlier unsanitary dumps, which had polluted the surface water of nearby settlements.

MDPs made significant improvements to urban transport. The municipality of Shanghai was able to complete its high-capacity inner ring road under **China II,** an operation like others in the country that paid little attention to public transport. Mostly through traffic management improvements, with construction limited to widening existing streets, **China III** introduced better traffic surveillance and monitoring to the city of Tianjin. Traffic management was a priority under **Vietnam II,** too, especially through the

successful introduction of computer-controlled traffic lights in Hanoi (population 1.4 million), which led to average trip time savings of 30 percent, well above the 10 percent targeted.

Compared with other Regions, MDP coverage of slum upgrading was thin, although **Philippines I** supported investments in this area across 74 municipalities. This focus was also found under **Indonesia V** in Kalimantan. The most successful component of the latter MDP was the **Kampung Improvement Program** in five municipalities, a program component that the Bank has supported for more than two decades throughout the country. In contrast, an activity supported in East Asia but not found often elsewhere was the support under **China I** that enabled twice the coverage by Beijing's interconnected district heating network.

Services—Private provision

Very few MDPs focused attention on expanding the role of the private sector in providing municipal services. Consequently, IEG found few examples of significant results in this area within the Region. Efforts were made through some MDPs to stimulate private commercial operations in service delivery by closing old municipal service departments and replacing them with agencies, such as the Beijing Drainage Company under **China I** and the Shanghai Public Transport Company under **China II,** but these new enterprises remained firmly harnessed to the state sector. The first steps toward a private-public partnership in water supply at the municipal level were taken in Shandong Province under **China XIII.**

Income level of beneficiaries—Poverty reduction

Few MDPs in the Region—mostly those in Indonesia and the Philippines—focused clearly on the urban poor. **Indonesia VIII,** for instance, supported 18,000 infrastructure microprojects that had been identified by participatory community development plans in low-income urban areas. **Indonesia V,** particularly through its *kampung* improvement program of upgrading low-income areas with basic services, is estimated to have benefited nearly half the population of the

---

Box C.1: Key to MDPs Referred to in Text

China: I—Beijing Environment; II—Shanghai Metropolitan Transport; III—Tianjin Urban Development Project; IV—Zhejiang Multicities Development; V—Southern Jiangsu Environmental Protection; VI—Shanghai Environment; VII—Second Shanghai Metropolitan Transport; VIII—Liaoning Environment; IX—Enterprise Housing and Social Security Reform; X—Yunnan Environment; XI—Hubei Urban Environment; XII—Chongqing Industrial Pollution Control and Reform; XIII—Shandong Environment; XIV—Liaoning Urban Transport; XV—Sichuan Urban Environment; XVI—Chongqing Urban Environment; XVII—Urumqi Urban Transport; XVIII—Shijiazhuang Urban Transport; XIX—Tianjin Second Urban Development; XX—Wuhan Urban Transport; XXI—Chongqing Small Cities Infrastructure Improvement; XXII—Liuzhou Environment Management; XXIII—Second Shang-

hai Urban (APL). **Indonesia:** I—Sulawesi–Irian Jaya Urban Development; II—East Java/Bali Urban Development; III—Semarang Surakarta Urban Development; IV—Surabaya Urban Development; V—Kalimantan Urban Development; VI—Second East Java Urban Development; VII—Second Sulawesi Urban Development; VIII—Urban Poverty; IX—Municipal Innovations; X—Western Java Environmental Management; XI—Second Urban Poverty; XII—Urban Sector Development and Reform. **Korea:** Pusan Urban Transport. **Mongolia:** Urban Services Improvement. **Philippines:** I—Third Municipal Development; II—Local Government Unit Finance and Development; III—Support for Strategic Local Development and Investment. **Vietnam:** I—Water Supply; II—Urban Transport Improvement; III—Urban Upgrading; IV—Coastal Cities Environmental Sanitation.

Source: IEG.

---

five client municipalities in Kalimantan. **Philippines I** started out with a strong focus on benefiting the poor, but this became less clear in the face of incentives for municipalities to embark on revenue-generating subprojects that would benefit higher-income groups.

Conclusions

- In countries with unitary municipal administrations for very large cities (even megacities), such as China, the retail approach to strengthening municipal management can be an appropriate model.

- MDPs have enabled many municipalities to strengthen their management of service provision, especially for improving the urban environment. The sectoral focus varies across countries in the Region, pointing to possibilities of fruitful exchanges of successful experiences among them.

- Results in strengthening municipal finances have been less evident across this Region, calling for more MDP efforts to enhance revenue mobilization for municipalities to fund the O&M necessary to sustain the service provision achievements obtained thus far.

Bank Support

More than 280 million people live in cities in the Europe and Central Asia Region—64 percent of the total population. Through 28 MDPs active during the 1998–2008 decade, the World Bank made commitments of $1.7 billion. This portfolio aimed to strengthen the management of 292 municipalities in 16 countries. By number of MDPs, the most active borrowers were the Russian Federation (4 projects), Bosnia and Herzegovina (4), Georgia (3), Turkey (3), Kazakhstan (2), and the Kyrgyz Republic (2). The remaining 10—Armenia, Croatia, Kosovo, Latvia, Lithuania, Poland, Tajikistan, Turkmenistan, Ukraine, and Uzbekistan—hosted 1 MDP each. Thus, half of the Region's MDPs were in upper-middle-income countries. Countries in the Region with large urban populations but no Bank-financed MDPs are Romania and Belarus.

Portfolio Performance

Sixty-three percent of completed MDPs achieved satisfactory outcomes, and the percentage of satisfactory Bank and borrower performance was a little higher. These figures are somewhat below the Bank-wide averages.

Among successful cases in the Region's portfolio, **Russia IV** stands out for its outcome rating of highly satisfactory. The project considerably strengthened the financial management of the newly created municipality of Kazan (population 1.2 million) by helping local officials organize and unify municipal accounts, debts, and other obligations. The municipality turned a deficit into a small surplus. Outstanding payables, a major problem at the outset, were substantially reduced. Two-thirds of the project funding was used for urgent repairs to abandoned and

Table D.1: Summary of MDP Portfolio, 1998–2008	
Completed (number)	16
Completed MDPs (% satisfactory)	63
Ongoing MDPs (number)	12
IBRD commitments (US$ million)	1,496
IDA commitments (US$ million)	207
Bank commitments per completed MDP (US$ million)	36
Commitments per ongoing MDP (US$ million)	94
Wholesale MDPs (number)	6
Retail MDPs (number)	22
Countries served (number)	16
Municipalities served (number)	292

Source: World Bank data.
Note: IBRD = International Bank for Reconstruction and Development; IDA = International Development Association; MDP = municipal development project.

derelict schools and health centers, bringing them back into full use. Kazan considerably improved its asset management, divesting some unnecessary inventory. Real estate assets remaining on the municipal books are now leased at 90 percent of their market values, up from 50 percent prior to the project.

Other successful examples included **Bosnia and Herzegovina I,** which helped develop a municipal credit market as intended. In the process, it strengthened financial management both by the municipalities and by five commercial banks that entered this market for the first time, making 28 loans for $13.3 million.

Turkey I helped improve the efficiency of water use in municipalities by substantially improving worker productivity per connection as well as the bill-collection ratio. The **Kyrgyz Republic** project

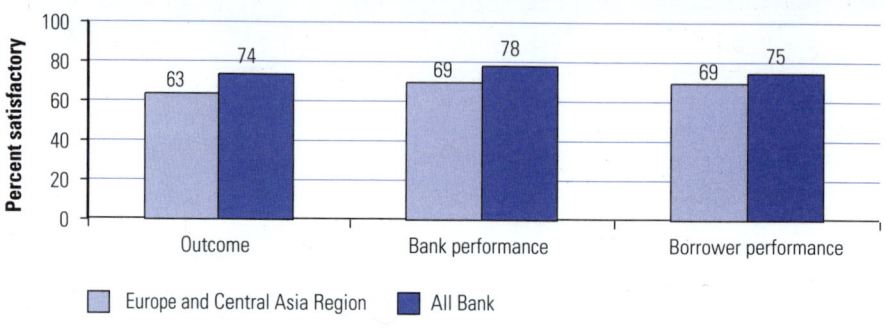

Figure D.1: MDP Portfolio Performance, Fiscal 1998–2008

Source: IEG special study.

Note: MDP = municipal development project.

was successful in separating road planning, budgeting, and contract administration from road construction, as intended, and it helped the municipalities of Jalalabad, Bishkek, and Osh set up their own passenger transport authorities to plan, contract, and monitor the private provision of local services. **Georgia III** helped nine municipalities, housing three-quarters of the country's urban population, to become creditworthy and particularly increased the effectiveness of their delivery of street paving and water supply services.

At the same time, three MDPs turned in a weak performance. The **Poland MDP** had little impact on the development of a commercial credit market for municipal investment. Its performance was undermined by a 1999 Finance Law that prevented municipal borrowing, and the project disbursed very little. The **Kazakhstan** project failed to promote efficient municipal management of social assets divested by state-owned enterprises, mainly because the project gave insufficient attention to the financial challenges the municipalities faced. The **Lithuania MDP** did not strengthen municipal management, as intended, because the Association of Local Authorities of Lithuania, slated as the executing agency for the project, lacked the necessary capability and resources to perform this function effectively.

Better City Planning

More information

Few MDPs in the Region aimed specifically to strengthen information systems for municipal management and planning. But the need for such information was acute in **Georgia** in the mid-1990s; three successive MDPs in that country introduced computer equipment and made municipal information more transparent under the law. However, much progress remains to be made, and Georgia can learn from other good experiences, such as Chile's Information System on Municipalities. **Russia I** successfully created a territorial information and analytic system for land, real estate, and infrastructure and a developer's manual, both of which have

Table D.2: Municipal Management Focus of Region Portfolio

Share of all MDPs with a project design focus on:	Completed	Ongoing
City planning		
In objectives (%)	25	33
In components (%)	56	67
Municipal finance		
In objectives (%)	75	25
In components (%)	75	92
Service delivery		
In objectives (%)	88	83
In components (%)	81	92
Number of all MDPs	16	12

Source: IEG special study.

Note: MDP = municipal development project.

had a positive impact on the housing market and have become valuable references for potential foreign investors and other parties.

Monitoring and evaluation

M&E design in MDPs, as for many other projects, was often weak because it focused on the delivery of component outputs rather than achieving project outcomes. Even some output indicators were not always clear or measurable, lacking baseline and endline (target) data. This prevented M&E implementation and use as a feedback mechanism to inform and improve project performance. M&E in the **Latvia** and **Kosovo** projects did not distinguish between output and outcome indicators. These projects especially lacked those indicators that could measure actual institutional improvements against those planned and relied too heavily on users' opinions, expressed through beneficiary assessments. Performance indicators could not be measured for lack of data—for example, on municipal action plans in the **Kyrgyz Republic MDP** or on municipal finances under the first Georgia MDP. During **Georgia II** and **III**, M&E focused more on management information on municipalities, and this information slowly became available in the country. The lack of baseline data undermined the effectiveness of M&E in the **Turkey MDP**, which did not explicitly cite preproject levels of pollution in the Sea of Marmara, for instance.

The **Kazakh MDP's** M&E could not capitalize on technical assistance relating to financial management methods and was unable to produce monitoring data on a continuous basis to measure its operating performance. **Russia IV** in Kazan, in contrast, incorporated a strong M&E system, whose design included easy-to-measure indicators such as municipal debt and level of targeted cash-transfer subsidies that were also part of the conditions of tranche release of the structural adjustment design of this loan.

Urban and spatial planning

Most MDPs in the Region did not include significant urban planning activities. An exception was **Russia I** in St. Petersburg, which drafted several laws to aid the planning process in improving the availability of serviced land. The laws had yet to be ratified at the time of project completion.

Investment planning and strategies

By training 550 staff in 30 municipalities, **Kosovo's MDP** helped prepare five-year rolling financial plans for the first time and incorporated community inputs through participatory processes. The **Kyrgyz Republic MDP** helped Jalalabad and Bishkek municipalities prepare plans for financing and contracting urban road building, which was separate from the construction itself.

Stronger Municipal Finances

Better financial management

Several MDPs achieved positive results in this area. Among the most notable was **Russia IV** in Kazan, where project technical assistance helped local staff unify the municipal accounts for the first time and make them more transparent. Among other things, computerized accounts allowed Kazan's employees to receive their salaries on time.

Other experiences show that equipment, technical assistance, or training alone is not enough to ensure better financial management. Initially, municipalities made limited use of computing equipment provided through **Georgia I. Uzbekistan's MDP** did not lead to improved financial management by the municipal solid waste utility, despite the technical assistance provided. The actual modernization of municipal management did not occur in the **Turkmenistan's MDP** without the widely expected devolution of responsibilities to the local level. Under the **Kazakhstan** project, municipal water utilities did not implement modern financial management techniques, for which training was provided, because of discontinuities in leadership. Similar weaknesses in the **Latvia MDP** were partly overcome by twinning the Daugavpils city water utility with the water works of the city of Tampere in Finland.

Mobilizing own revenues

The Region's MDP portfolio obtained some good results in this area. Technical assistance through

Bank supervision of **Russia IV** helped Kazan find alternative sources of revenue, which were urgently needed, as large federal transfers were soon to lapse. Municipalities participating in **Georgia II** increased own-source revenues by 11 percent during 1998–2002, compared with a decrease of 16 percent for other municipalities, thanks in part to the incentives to become creditworthy.

The **Kyrgyz Republic MDP** helped establish urban road funds and raised taxes threefold on private vehicles. The **Uzbekistan MDP** did not succeed in establishing a stable self-financing mechanism for solid waste management through planned tariff adjustments, although a last-minute reprieve prevented the operation's collapse. Specific cost recovery from MDP investments themselves obtained good results in the **Turkey MDP,** where the Bursa municipal water and sanitation utility successfully maintained tariffs at levels sufficient to meet its financial obligations.

Municipal creditworthiness and debt management

Under **Georgia I** the Municipal Development Fund of Georgia became Georgia's main funding source for municipalities and an instrument for strengthening municipal management. Today the fund has become the government's principal agency for financing major development programs beyond just municipal development. The latest **Georgia III** project saw 9 municipalities, home to 73 percent of the urban population, become creditworthy, also giving some of them access to additional concessional funding. Under the previous **Georgia II,** some municipalities had overborrowed and defaulted on their loan repayments.

Technical assistance to 32 municipalities and, most significantly, to 5 commercial banks under **Bosnia and Herzegovina I** helped municipalities become more creditworthy by increasing revenue collections and helping banks understand their debt portfolio better. The government supported a similar approach under the **Kyrgyz Republic MDP,** partly in the hope of reducing the financial burden of subsidies. The

potential foreign exchange risk inherent in external funding of municipal credit does not appear to have constrained municipal creditworthiness in the Region. In Poland, with memories of that country's recent high inflation, commercial banks tried unsuccessfully to transfer this risk to equally reluctant municipalities, stalling project implementation. But in most other countries, central governments and their agents have been willing to assume this risk.

Private finance participation

To date, MDP efforts and results in getting private finance into municipal services have been limited. Poland's project did not succeed in channeling private bank funds into municipalities because of the overall project failure. Private funding of Tashkent's solid waste management under **Uzbekistan's MDP** could not proceed while the operation continued to operate at a loss. Private funding of Kazan's water utility under **Russia IV** was held back because the public operator received support from other donors.

Improved Service Provision

Investment priorities

As in other Regions and sectors, few MDPs gave much attention to estimating ERRs, either at appraisal or at completion. To be eligible for project financing, **Bosnia and Herzegovina I** did require participating municipalities to demonstrate that subprojects achieved at least 12 percent ERR, but information on the actual rates achieved was not systematically monitored. After a poor start in neglecting ERR estimates in its earlier projects, **Georgia III** ensured that all subprojects met minimum rates of return. The **Kyrgyz Republic MDP** also reported, thanks to huge savings in operating costs, high ERRs for its urban road investments in Bishkek, Jalalabad, and Osh.

Although the project itself was barely implemented, the **Poland MDP** did lead commercial banks to require that municipalities' proposals for subprojects meet minimum ERR requirements. Unconvincing reasons for the lack of ERR estimates in this Region are similar to those given in other Regions, such as Bank guidelines not requiring them for emergency projects and lines of credit.

Procurement

Several MDPs gave municipalities a first opportunity to become involved in the competitive procurement of works and services, with some positive results. Under **Russia IV,** Kazan municipality voluntarily adopted local competitive bidding—not required with a structural adjustment loan—which resulted in lower-price contracts. Sole-source purchasing was reduced from 55 percent of total to 25 percent, which was better than the target of 35 percent.

The **Uzbekistan** project introduced international competitive bidding to Tashkent municipality that resulted in significant cost savings in the acquisition of a new fleet of 270 solid waste collection vehicles. **Georgia III** enabled municipalities to play a greater role in procurement than had been possible under the earlier operations, although local management there still needs to be strengthened more. More centralized political arrangements in some of the Region's countries leave procurement as a government responsibility.

Operations and maintenance

There was little evidence of MDP attention to ongoing O&M. In the **Kyrgyz Republic MDP,** however, each participating municipality had to adopt a prioritized five-year road maintenance program for its urban roads and streets. The **Uzbekistan MDP** established a repair and maintenance depot, generously equipped with spare parts at the outset, to keep the fleet of new solid waste collection vehicles on the road. Under the **Latvia MDP,** the lack of such a facility put the vehicles of one major Riga bus company at risk.

Services—Most affected sectors

Among all activities undertaken, the projects performed best in improving services and related infrastructure, especially for urban street paving and drainage, neighborhood upgrading, and basic sanitation and other environmental improvements. **Georgia II** successfully completed 89 subprojects in 11 municipalities, with two-thirds of project investment in Tbilisi and three-fourths of investments in road rehabilitation and water supply. The greatest improvements were in urban road paving and clearing blocked drainage that caused periodic flooding.

Under **Georgia I,** during the country's post-independence phase, infrastructure and services were preserved and improved for power, heating, and water. The Tbilisi Metro, which is used by 90 percent of the city's population, was "rescued" through the emergency funding of signaling systems and spare parts. Dysfunctional sewerage systems in the municipalities of Batumi and Poti were restored to working order, though service levels were still short of desired goals. Restoring heating to hospitals and school buildings in five municipalities allowed continued operation throughout the winter.

The **Kazakhstan** project allowed the water utility to supply good quality drinking water to 37,000 people in two municipalities. The project's cleanup of sewage spills had an immediate health impact: between 1999 and 2002, the number of dysentery cases fell from 83 to 8, and typhoid cases fell from 83 to 0. According to the beneficiary assessment of the **Kosovo MDP,** 90 percent of respondents felt that the 115 (mostly school and water supply) subprojects implemented in 30 municipalities did respond to their needs; 84 percent were satisfied with results that they felt helped reduce water-borne diseases.

The **Kyrgyz Republic** project exceeded its target by substantially improving 105 kilometers of roads, making the municipalities of Jalalabad, Bishkek, and Osh more accessible. **Latvia's MDP** helped improve drinking water quality, and untreated water was no longer being discharged into the Daugava River. The **Lithuania MDP** contributed only modestly to improvement in conditions of municipal service infrastructure, but it did help reduce street lighting energy costs in Vilnius. The **Turkmenistan** project helped increase bus and trolley services in Ashgabat, fully meeting targets, as well as contributing to enhanced reliability and frequency of services.

Box D.1: Key to MDPs Referred to in Text

Armenia: Third Social Investment Fund Project. **Bosnia and Herzegovina:** I—Local Development Project; II—Community Development Project; III—Solid Waste Management Project; IV—Urban Infrastructure & Services Project. **Croatia:** Coastal Cities Pollution Control Project. **Georgia:** I—Municipal Infrastructure Rehabilitation Project; II—Municipal Development Project; III—Second Municipal Development & Decentralization Project. **Kazakhstan:** I—Social Protection Project; II—Atyrau Pilot Water. **Kosovo:** Second Community Development Fund. **Kyrgyz Republic:** I—Urban Transport Project; II—Small Towns Infrastructure & Capacity Building Project. **Latvia:** Municipal Services Development Project. **Lithuania:** Municipal Development Project. **Poland:** Municipal Finance Project. **Russia:** I—St. Petersburg Center City Rehabilitation Project; II—Northern Restructuring Project; III—St. Petersburg Economic Development Project; IV—Kazan Municipal Development Project. **Tajikistan:** Municipal Infrastructure Project. **Turkey:** I—Bursa Water & Sanitation Project; II—Municipal Services Project; III—Istanbul Municipal Infrastructure Project. **Turkmenistan:** Urban Transport Project. **Ukraine:** Urban Infrastructure Project. **Uzbekistan:** Tashkent Solid Waste Management Project.

Source: IEG.

Wastewater collection systems and networks with 80 percent treatment were put in place in Bursa city under **Turkey I,** which led to increased service coverage between 1993 and 2000—from 93 percent to 97 percent of the population for water supply and from 73 percent to 82 percent for sewerage. Over the same period, unaccounted-for water fell from 65 percent to 45 percent. **Uzbekistan** obtained positive environmental results by helping restore Tashkent's solid waste management system. For the most part, the environmental impacts of roads, water, and solid waste subprojects of **Georgia I–III** were positive, especially through improving air and water quality in the poorer neighborhoods of the beneficiary municipalities.

Services—Private provision

Private provision of services was relatively low among this Region's MDPs. The **Kyrgyz Republic MDP** helped three municipalities—Jalalabad, Bishkek, and Osh—establish passenger transport authorities and plan, contract, and monitor the private provision of services. Construction is now awarded to private contractors, and major equipment has been sold to the private sector.

Under **Turkey I,** the Bursa Metropolitan Municipality contracted waste collection and landfill operations to private contractors. It also promoted private participation for meter reading, billing, and invoicing. The **Turkmenistan MDP** helped increase private participation of the suburban and intercity transport to 70 percent, but greater effort could have been made at deregulation, to allow greater competition. Under the **Uzbekistan** project, an international tender in 2003 for the private operation of Makhsustrans's Chilanzar and Shaihantaur districts of Tashkent failed to yield any bids because of doubts about the profitability of the operations without subsidies.

Income level of beneficiaries—Poverty reduction

Only four MDPs have explicit poverty-reduction objectives. The **Kosovo MDP** broadly met its Regional poverty goals. The project directed the majority of its social services toward the disabled, women, and youth and generated 26,188 days of temporary employment. But there is less evidence on outreach to other vulnerable groups such as widows, victims of conflict, inhabitants of remote villages, and so forth.

Under **Russia IV** in Kazan, the newly created Municipal Department of Social Protection identified eligible poor recipients through the municipality's new computerized database of 23,900 assisted families to replace earlier untargeted subsidies with direct cash payments, which also produced an overall savings to the municipality.

Several "one-stop shops" were created to provide these services to the beneficiaries.

Conclusions

- By continuing to do more wholesale MDPs that emulate the successful cases in this Region, positive MDP impact can be broadened to benefit more municipalities.

- New MDPs could make better and more intensive use of simple ERR estimates to determine investment priorities and measure efficiency of results.
- M&E of new MDPs needs to be stronger than in the past, especially in measuring the achievement of objectives through quantified baselines and targets.

APPENDIX E: BANKING ON MUNICIPALITIES: WORLD BANK SUPPORT IN LATIN AMERICA AND THE CARIBBEAN

Bank Support

Latin America and the Caribbean is the most urbanized of the Bank's Regions. Currently, some 435 million people, 78 percent of the total population, live in cities. The urban population now grows at only half the annual rate of the 1970s.

During the past decade (1998–2008), the World Bank had a portfolio of 36 active MDPs and committed $2.6 billion to them. The Region's MDPs aimed to strengthen the management of 1,098 municipalities in 13 countries. The most active borrowers were Colombia (7 projects), Brazil (5), Honduras (4), Venezuela (3), Peru (3), and Argentina (3). Mexico, Ecuador, Chile, Bolivia, Nicaragua, Haiti, and Belize had 1 or 2 projects each. Half the MDPs were in higher-middle-income countries; the other half—except Haiti (low-income)—were in lower-middle-income countries. The Region's MDP portfolio covered all countries in the Region with large urban populations.

Portfolio Performance

The Region's MDP portfolio has a strong performance record, with 86 percent of completed operations rated satisfactory. This Region reports the best MDP performance among the six Bank Regions.

An outstanding performer, rated highly satisfactory, was **Colombia II.** It successfully strengthened the capacity of institutions in charge of planning, managing, and maintaining urban transport infrastructure in Bogotá (population 7.1 million). This MDP lowered sector administration costs from 17 percent in 1996 to 10 percent in 1998, and road maintenance costs

Table E.1: Summary of MDP Portfolio, 1998–2008	
Completed MDPs (number)	21
Completed MDPs (% satisfactory)	86
Ongoing MDPs (number)	15
IBRD commitments (US$m)	2,485
IDA commitments (US$m)	166
Commitments per completed MDP (US$ million)	86
Commitments per ongoing MDP (US$ million)	56
Wholesale MDPs (number)	16
Retail MDPs (number)	20
Countries served (number)	13
Municipalities served (number)	1,098

Source: World Bank data.
Note: IBRD = International Bank for Reconstruction and Development; IDA = International Development Association; MDP = municipal development project.

were lowered by 77 percent, despite a sevenfold increase in the network between 1996 and 1999.

Venezuela I introduced basic infrastructure on a large scale to low-income barrios in 45 municipalities across the country, benefiting 66,000 poor families; this was 43 percent above target. The project exposed these municipalities to lending operations for the first time, supporting their financial management and revenue growth through detailed technical assistance. **Colombia I** and its follow-on **Colombia IV** together helped create a local credit market among 179 municipalities around the country, although municipal demand for credit was weaker than expected. Municipalities with conservative financial administrations were reluctant to take on debt, and other creditworthy borrowers had alternative sources of credit. Between them, **Brazil I** and **III,** in the states of Minas Gerais and Bahia, respectively, brought technical assistance for improving

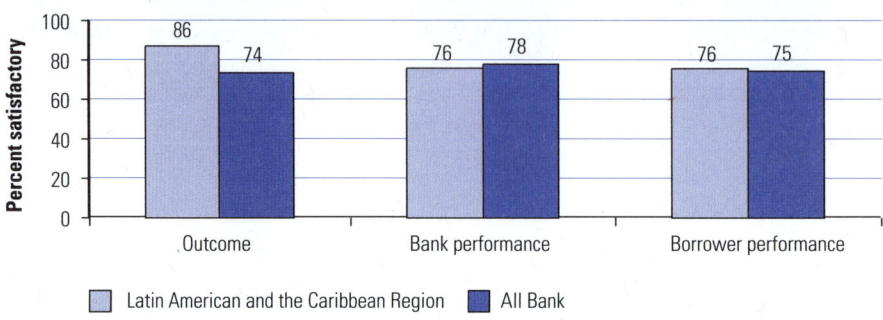

Figure E.1: MDP Portfolio Performance, Fiscal 1998–2008

Legend: Latin American and the Caribbean Region / All Bank

Source: IEG special study.
Note: MDP = municipal development project.

financial management to 179 municipalities, each using a wholesale arrangement through their state intermediaries.

Among the most important physical results obtained were improvements in the urban environment that were attained through basic sanitation investments financed by the projects. Valuable results in the form of a nationwide municipal information system came from **Chile II.** A wholesale operation on a larger scale involving 77 municipalities, the **Bolivia MDP** helped strengthen administrative and financial controls. It also focused physical investment on basic sanita-

tion in the poorer municipalities, especially in the Beni region. **Ecuador I** successfully helped make the fiscal transfers to municipalities more transparent, as intended, while helping improve the administrative efficiency of 99 municipalities throughout the country.

In contrast, three MDPs had unsatisfactory outcomes. The **Haiti** operation (retail) failed to expand the water supply to the capital Port au Prince or make it more efficient. Water metering targets were not met, and illegal consumption continued unabated. Most of the loan for **Mexico I** was cancelled, as six municipalities on the U.S. border region were unprepared to meet the project's environmental requirements, in compliance with the norms of the North American Free Trade Agreement. Deteriorating national economic conditions undermined the ability of **Mexico II** to finance the modern municipal solid waste landfills, although there was some progress in improving municipal planning of solid waste management, thanks to project technical assistance that went ahead. The Bank was slow to restructure the project, which resulted in the cancellation of 70 percent of the loan.

Better City Planning

More information

There were few instances in the Region of MDPs generating or using information for planning. Chile was a notable exception. **Chile I** and **II**

Table E.2: Municipal Management Focus of Region Portfolio		
Share of all MDPs with a project design focus on:	**Completed**	**Ongoing**
City planning		
In objectives (%)	43	33
In components (%)	24	87
Municipal finance		
In objectives (%)	71	20
In components (%)	43	47
Service delivery		
In objectives (%)	90	60
In components (%)	95	87
Number of all MDPs	21	15

Source: IEG special study.
Note: MDP = municipal development project.

launched and consolidated the National System for Municipal Information (SINIM), which has reported about the situation and performance through more than 250 indicators for all 345 municipalities since 2000. Available over the Internet, SINIM covers local finances, administration, health and education services, spatial planning, poverty, other social indicators, as well as geographic characteristics of all Chile's municipalities. But **Colombia III** failed to create a national environmental information system based on municipalities, because the Ministry of the Environment did not play the coordination role expected of it. **Brazil I** and **III,** in the respective states of Minas Gerais and Bahia, implemented similar databases at the state level and helped individual municipalities build their own information systems.

Most progress in compiling information was made by extending and consolidating local property tax registers, or cadastres. **Colombia II** improved these to such an extent that it exceeded its target of updating 4.5 million title registers by 57 percent. At the municipal level, performance in using the additional information for strong taxation flows varied.

Monitoring and evaluation

As in other Regions—and other sectors, too—MDPs in this Region obtained at best modest results in designing, implementing, and using M&E. The usual culprits were found: focus mainly on outputs rather than outcomes, lack of baseline data to compare against actual achievements, and inadequate collection of data on actual project performance.

Under **Argentina I,** a well-conceived logframe with performance indicators was established at midterm review for infrastructure works, but a similar effort for institutional development was less successful. Under **Brazil II,** the M&E framework to verify the achievement of project objectives was weak. Under **Brazil III,** three years after Board approval, the Bank and borrower agreed to adopt a set of indicators to monitor outputs and outcomes. However, actual outcome data appeared infrequently and

seemed inconsistent, providing only anecdotal evidence of increased tax-collection rates, improved health conditions, and improved access to water and sanitation services.

Under **Chile I,** a lack of M&E on outcomes meant that claims of strengthened municipal management as a result of project technical assistance on information technology could not be substantiated. Even **Chile II,** which otherwise excelled in providing information for planning, did poorly on M&E. Its design included 18 performance indicators, but these were mostly about the delivery of outputs, such as the number of municipalities served and the number of technical assistance contracts made. The two indicators that came closest to monitoring achievement of project objectives were those that considered municipal own-source revenues and municipal operational surpluses.

Honduras also lacked explicit and quantifiable indicators able to demonstrate progress toward sustained coastal tourism in the project region. For **Mexico II,** the logframe developed during supervision was specified only in broad terms. The Implementation and Completion and Results Report cites several examples of project outputs used to justify conclusions on outcomes. **Venezuela II** lacked appropriate performance indicators altogether, but **Venezuela III** paid more attention to the design of the M&E system. However, it was barely used, as baseline data were not collected because of lack of inadequate resources.

Urban and spatial planning

Although nine MDPs had objectives focused on strengthening municipal planning, there is little evidence of what was actually achieved. **Colombia III** led to the preparation of 17 municipal environmental plans and the incorporation of environmental aspects into land-use plans.

Investment planning and strategies

IEG found limited evidence of achievements in this area. One reported instance was **Argentina I,** which helped many municipalities plan cost-effective investment programs.

Stronger Municipal Finances

Better financial management

The majority of MDPs in this Region aimed to improve municipalities' financial management, starting with better accounting and financial reporting systems. On balance, the results from these efforts have been positive, sometimes with valuable demonstration effects on municipalities that were not part of the projects. **Bolivia I** helped 77 municipalities strengthen their financial control systems.

Brazil I in Minas Gerais provided technical assistance for financial management to about 50 municipalities, a good number but well short of the ambitious plans to cover all urban municipalities in the state. Under **Chile I,** municipal practices and technical capacity have been improved, and equipment (computers, communications, drivers' license testing) has been updated. Similar improvements were reported under **Mexico I.** In addition, **Venezuela I** provided on-the-job learning opportunities for 45 municipalities to manage credit operations for the first time.

Mobilizing own revenues

Through technical assistance, **Bolivia I** municipalities improved their resource mobilization. **Brazil II** reported that 26 municipalities assisted by the project increased their own revenues more than other municipalities, but IEG found the statistical significance of this evidence questionable.

More significant is that own revenues for project municipalities grew faster than higher-level transfers over the 2001–03 period. Under **Brazil III,** a survey indicated that the majority of participating municipalities increased efficiency in financial management and tax administration and showed a sustained increase in the collection of property taxes and services between 1996 and 2000. Under **Ecuador I,** of a random sample of 99 municipalities, 53 percent had doubled revenues in real terms over the project period.

Municipal creditworthiness and debt management

Several MDPs successfully introduced municipal-ities to credit operations, providing them with assistance for managing such operations. In particular, **Colombia I** and **IV** effectively established a local credit market with the official Local Development Fund, called FINDETER; this currently has a credit rating of AAA, refinancing commercial bank loans to municipalities to fund their investments in infrastructure and services. One municipality, Pereira (population 0.4 million), was able to issue bonds that were oversubscribed, and another (Barranquilla, population 1.4 million) was able to pay off its short-term debt thanks to project advice on portfolio management.

Brazil I, II, and **III** enhanced the credit management capabilities of poor municipalities especially, as did **Ecuador I.** But such efforts to consolidate local credit in the Region have been thwarted in recent years by national efforts to control fiscal deficits at the local level. In Chile, borrowing by municipalities is forbidden altogether.

Private finance participation

Progress in this direction was not widely achieved through MDPs. **Colombia IV,** however, helped municipalities increase water, gas, and solid waste tariffs, for instance, making some services profitable for private investors. This situation continues to this day, although services are less affordable to the poor. Average household expenditure on basic sanitation rose by 204 percent between 1997 and 2003. Attempts to stimulate private funding and operation of municipalities made little headway under **Brazil I** and **III,** mainly because of a lack of interest by the municipalities themselves. **Venezuela II** found a similar reluctance toward privatization of urban transport.

Improved Service Provision

Investment priorities

About half the completed MDPs reported ERR estimates at appraisal and completion. High ERRs (34–42 percent) at completion were estimated for basic sanitation and slum upgrading investments under **Venezuela III** and **Brazil I** and **III.**

Strong ERRs (29–34 percent) were also reported for municipal urban transport investments under **Colombia II** and **Venezuela II.** MDPs that did not report internal rates of return at completion included **Mexico I** and **II, Ecuador I** and **II, Argentina I,** and **Honduras II.** Operations such as these, which included investment in municipal infrastructure and services, would have been amenable to simple estimates of ERRs that would have informed the evaluation about performance efficiency.

Procurement

With long histories of decentralized municipal responsibilities, many municipalities have significant experience with managing procurement. Nevertheless, **Brazil II** did introduce 49 poorer municipalities in the state of Ceará to handling competitive procurement for works. Similarly, **Venezuela I** helped 45 municipalities learn to manage procurement themselves as decentralization gathered pace in that country.

Operations and maintenance

Although municipalities are typically responsible for O&M of infrastructure and services within their jurisdictions, few MDPs paid attention to this aspect of municipal management. One exception was **Venezuela I's** provision of technical assistance and training to participating municipalities for carrying out urban road maintenance activities, affecting 360 kilometers of pavement. Another was **Venezuela III,** which tried to build up local O&M capabilities but came up against municipalities' unwillingness to curtail investments by allocating more resources to O&M, especially at times of financial crisis in the capital Caracas (population 1.8 million).

Services—Most affected sectors

As in other Regions, the most popular services provided through MDPs included urban transport, slum upgrading, basic sanitation, solid waste management, and other urban environmental improvements.

Municipalities were able to improve urban transport through MDPs across the Region. **Colombia II,** for instance, brought the very

successful *Transmilenio* bus-operated public transport to Bogotá (population 7.2 million), leading other municipalities, including Barranquilla (population 1.4 million), Pereira (population 0.4 million), and Cali (population 2.4 million), to plan similar bus projects. There was also interest from other countries. Through financing and training of 250 municipal staff, **Venezuela II** enabled municipalities to make simple traffic management improvements such as road signals, intersection improvements, and rationalization of bus routes to reduce traffic congestion. In **Belize,** street and traffic improvements—including traffic signal systems, improved street drainage, widened sidewalks for pedestrians, and bicycle lanes—had a positive impact on road safety.

According to two surveys made at the completion of **Brazil III,** respiratory and intestinal diseases were reduced in municipalities in Bahia state in low-income areas where street paving had reduced dust particles and basic sanitation had prevented the pollution of the water supply by sewage. In contrast, sewage treatment remains a major challenge in the Region. Pereira is still without sewage treatment for its 440,000 inhabitants, who live in an ecologically sensitive zone, despite the successful participation of the municipality in several projects, including **Colombia I.** Similar shortcomings in final sewage treatment were evident under **Brazil I,** which nevertheless brought other basic sanitation improvements to 150 municipalities in the state of Minas Gerais. The introduction of the final disposal and treatment facilities for solid waste proved challenging under **Mexico II,** where deteriorating macroeconomic conditions meant that only three of the seven facilities intended were built, and only partially.

Other urban environmental improvements introduced by MDPs included, in **Colombia II,** controls over discarding used tires and batteries, as well as the reduction of noise pollution by urban traffic through the deployment and use of new monitoring equipment. Other MDPs helped reinforce municipal management of the urban environment. Thus, **Colombia III** helped 17 municipalities prepare environmental plans, and

Box E.1: Key to MDPs Referred to in Text

Argentina: I—Second Municipal Development; II—Basic Municipal Services; III—Subnational Government Public Sector Modernization. **Belize:** Belize City Infrastructure. **Bolivia:** I—Municipal Development; II—Urban Infrastructure. **Brazil:** I—Minas Municipal Development; II—Ceará Urban Development & Water Resource; III—Bahia Municipal Infrastructure Development & Management; IV—Bahia Poor Urban Areas Integrated Development; V—Recife Municipal APL. **Chile:** I—Municipal Development; II—Second Municipal Development. **Colombia:** I—Municipal Development; II—Bogota Urban Transport; III—Urban Environment; IV—Urban Infrastructure Services Development; V—Bogota Urban Services Project; VI—Integrated Mass Transit Systems; VII—Disaster Vulnerability Reduction Project. **Ecuador:** I—First Municipal Development; II—Environmental Management. **Haiti:** Port-au-Prince Water Supply. **Honduras:** I—Natural Disaster Mitigation; II—Sustainable Coastal Tourism Project; III—Barrio Ciudad; IV—Water & Sanitation Program. **Mexico:** I—Northern Border Environment; II—Solid Waste. **Nicaragua:** Natural Disaster Vulnerability Reduction. **Peru:** I—Lima Transport; II—Vilcanota Valley Rehabilitation & Management; III—Second Real Property Rights. **Venezuela:** I—Low-Income Barrios Improvement; II—Urban Transport; III—Caracas Slum Upgrading.

Source: IEG.

the **Ecuador MDP** helped 23 municipalities establish specific Environmental Management Units within their municipal administrations.

Income levels of beneficiaries—Poverty reduction

About one-third of MDPs in the Region had objectives explicitly focused on assisting the urban poor. Even for **Argentina I,** an MDP that was not specifically poverty focused, about one-fifth of the beneficiaries were poor. **Bolivia I,** which emphasized beneficiary participation in the choice of investments, made most investments in municipalities where poor people lived, such as in the Beni region of the Amazon.

Under **Brazil I,** municipalities in Minas Gerais state invested in lower-standard basic sanitation and upgrading only of interest to lower-income groups. **Brazil III** went one stage further in urban poverty mapping of the changes brought about by municipal investment in street paving, provision of drainage, and water supply and sanitation; however, the mapping was discontinued because of lack of resources. The poverty impact of **Colombia I's** work with 179 municipalities can be inferred from national data, which show that service coverage for those in the lowest quintile of income distribution improved significantly between 1993 and 2003, from 80 percent to 91 percent for electricity, 77

percent to 83 percent for basic sanitation, and 18 percent to 33 percent for fixed-line telephones. **Colombia II** survey data showed that most users of the *Transmilenio* urban transport system in Bogotá are within the two lowest quintiles.

Conclusions

- Doing more wholesale MDPs and scaling them up is likely to yield positive results in a Region where 100 percent of wholesale MDPs obtained satisfactory outcomes.

- More can be done to disseminate the good MDP practices in the Region. Globally, municipalities in other Regions could benefit from this experience in municipal information systems, municipal creditworthiness and financial management, urban transport, and poverty reduction. Within the Region itself, the Bank is poised to share MDP experiences among borrower countries. Finally, within individual countries, national and state authorities have opportunities to share and exchange experiences among municipalities from different parts.

- Successful experience from other Regions can be put to good use in those areas where shortcomings have been noted in the Region, such as in M&E, private financing of municipal services, O&M, and key environmental services, such as sewage and solid waste disposal and treatment.

APPENDIX F: BANKING ON MUNICIPALITIES:
WORLD BANK SUPPORT IN THE MIDDLE EAST AND NORTH AFRICA

Bank Support

About 180 million people live in cities in the Middle East and North Africa Region, about 57 percent of the total population. During the decade 1998–2008 the World Bank had a portfolio of 18 MDPs spanning 8 countries in the Region. The Bank commitments of $845 million focused on strengthening the municipal management of 379 municipalities in Tunisia (4 projects), West Bank and Gaza (4), the Republic of Yemen (3), Jordan (2), Lebanon (2), the Arab Republic of Egypt (1), the Islamic Republic of Iran (1), and Morocco (1). More than 70 percent of the projects are in lower-middle-income countries, 17 percent in low-income countries, and 11 percent in upper-middle-income countries. The Region's portfolio covered all countries in the Region with large urban populations (15 million plus) except for Algeria.

Portfolio Performance

Some 63 percent of completed MDPs in the Region achieved satisfactory outcomes. Bank performance was also satisfactory 63 percent of the time. These ratings are below Bank-wide averages. In contrast, 88 percent of MDPs have satisfactory borrower performance, well above the Bank average. The disconnect reflects good efforts by the borrower in West Bank and Gaza, where exogenous factors of conflict prevented commensurate project outcomes.

The strongest performing MDPs in the Region, each awarded satisfactory ratings for their outcomes and Bank and borrower performance, were in Tunisia and the West Bank and Gaza. **Tunisia I,** a wholesale operation assisting 257 municipalities throughout the country, produced

Table F.1: Summary of MDP Portfolio, 1998–2008

Completed (number)	8
Completed MDPs (% satisfactory)	63
Ongoing MDPs (number)	10
IBRD commitments (US$ million)	652
IDA commitments (US$ million)	94
Bank commitments per completed MDP (US$ million)	37
Commitments per ongoing MDP (US$ million)	55
Wholesale MDPs (number)	6
Retail MDPs (number)	12
Countries served (number)	8
Municipalities served (number)	379

Source: World Bank data.
Note: IBRD = International Bank for Reconstruction and Development; IDA = International Development Association; MDP = municipal development project.

excellent results that continue more than eight years after completion. Not only did MDP-participating municipalities increase their own revenues more than other municipalities, but the participants also produced a current surplus that was twice the target. The project helped the remote municipality of Kasserine (population 82,000) upgrade the Ezzouhour district of town and kept it in good condition through careful maintenance, sometimes involving local residents.

West Bank and Gaza III succeeded in meeting more modest objectives that focused on repairing municipal infrastructure damaged during the *intifada* rather than providing completely new services. Despite the difficult circumstances of its implementation, the project succeeded in making timely and effective repairs, thanks in part to strong and enthusiastic local leadership.

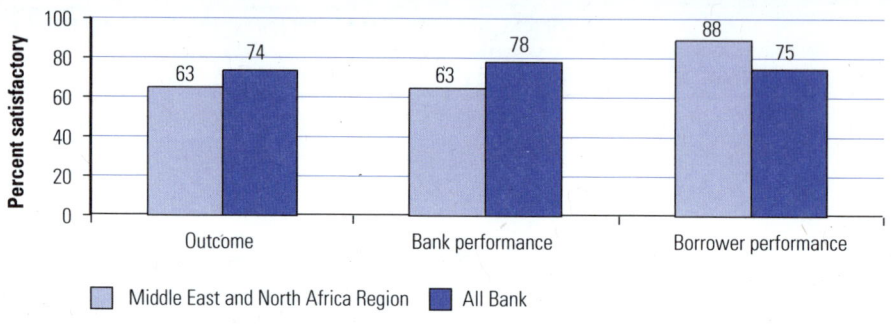

Figure F.1: MDP Portfolio Performance, Fiscal 1998–2008

Source: IEG special study.

Note: MDP = municipal development project.

Weaker performance was turned in by the **Morocco MDP,** which failed to improve the housing stock of the ancient city of Fez (population 964,891) as intended. Public-to-private leverage of investments for the rehabilitation of the Medina is likely to remain at a 1:1 ratio, well below the projected target of 1:13. However, the Fez municipality was consolidated through the amalgamation of six local governments around the time of project restructuring in 2003, and municipal management improved on the technical but not the financial side. **West Bank and Gaza I** also performed poorly. The start-up was at the time of the 2000 *intifada* and the Israeli military response to it. Because of events beyond the control of the project, the MDP was unable to assume any effective role in the national system of central and local government that the project hoped to constitute.

Better City Planning

More information

MDPs in the Region rarely set out to make more information available for municipal management. The best results were obtained under **Tunisia I,** although they could have been made more widely available to the municipalities themselves to help them improve their management. Instead, detailed information on municipal financial performance remained in the hands of the national Municipal Funding and Support Agency. A newer operation, **Jordan I** aims to improve information on municipal finances at the national level, as well as information for asset management at the municipal level, too.

Monitoring and evaluation

There is little information on the extent to which M&E frameworks were designed and used in projects in this Region. Wherever performance indicators were available, they mostly related to outputs (in the form of delivery of project components) rather than outcomes (in the form of achievement of project objectives). Even in such cases, baseline data were rarely available.

Table F.2: Municipal Management Focus of Region Portfolio

Share of all MDPs with a project design focus on:	Completed	Ongoing
City planning		
In objectives (%)	25	20
In components (%)	38	30
Municipal finance		
In objectives (%)	50	20
In components (%)	75	92
Service delivery		
In objectives (%)	100	70
In components (%)	100	80
Number of all MDPs	8	10

Source: IEG special study.

Note: MDP = municipal development project.

The **Republic of Yemen I,** for instance, did not have baseline data on before-project conditions to track the impact of new pipelines and household connections on improving water supply. In **Tunisia II's** M&E, the chosen performance indicators measured project outputs, such as the provision of project technical assistance, rather than moving toward the project objective of increasing the efficiency of public sector management at the municipal level, for which no baseline condition or targets were specified in the project design. IEG estimated that this project alone accounted for one quarter of all municipal investments in the country during the 1997–2003 period of its implementation. Despite this high profile, M&E was unable to show what impact the project had, only the levels of municipal services in the country as a whole.

West Bank and Gaza IV operated under the very difficult circumstances of the *intifada*. In the rush to plan and deliver emergency services at the outset, baseline indicators were not adequately set up. Overall, there was a persistent inadequacy of information about government processes, including budget and transfer data that should have improved under the project.

Urban and spatial planning
Little was achieved in strengthening municipal planning capabilities in the Region. Under **West Bank and Gaza I,** three municipalities prepared three-year development plans for the first time.

Investment planning and strategies
This too was not a common feature of MDPs in the Region. **Tunisia II** required 76 municipalities to prepare investment plans to be eligible for project funding of municipal infrastructure, but it is not clear how many actually did prepare them.

Stronger Municipal Finances

Better financial management
Under **Tunisia I** and **II** during 1993–2003, financial management by many of the 257

municipalities assisted by the projects improved, which led to better financial results. Stronger financial management was initially the outcome of rapid loan disbursements to finance priority local investments, which then progressed to the adoption of computerized accounting in 32 municipalities for the first time and to three-year budgeting and of outsourcing municipal services.

The municipality of Ariana (population 237,395) became one of the country's top 10 tax-collection districts—it ranks 23rd in population—after making its own tax administration more efficient, following intense training its officials had at the new municipal training center specially created by the project. Altogether, 10,000 local and central government staff received project training that covered more than 50 percent of all municipal staff in Tunisia at the time.

Under **Republic of Yemen I,** municipal management of the local water supply became a reality as the water authority of Sana'a (population 1.9 million) became a fully autonomous corporation able to cover operating costs for the first time in this sector; this also happened in 12 other municipalities. Municipal financial management began to improve under **West Bank and Gaza II,** as local governments began to institute solid waste collection fees, for instance, but the deteriorating security situation after 2000 stalled further progress.

Mobilizing own revenues
Tunisia I produced excellent results that continue to this day. Not only did participating municipalities increase their own revenues more than other municipalities, but the participants produced current surpluses that were twice the target. In the municipality of Monastir (population 64,222), for instance, municipal own revenues as a share of the total rose from 30 percent to 38 percent between 1991 and 1998. Resources for Tunisian municipalities enabled them to finance more investments than initially expected. Under **Tunisia II,** several municipalities were able to use these additional revenues to pay off short-term debts and build up net

savings. **Morocco's MDP** helped improve cost recovery and contributed to mobilizing internal and external resources in a nondeficit, noninflationary way to help finance minor investments by the municipality of Fez. This was a positive result for a project that otherwise failed to achieve its objectives.

Municipal creditworthiness and debt management

Tunisia I introduced 257 municipalities to the management of credit. As the agency responsible for implementing the project and collecting municipal debt service, the Municipal Funding and Support Agency saw its own creditworthiness enhanced when it obtained a credit rating of AA+ and successfully issued its own bonds in the local market, to the value of $23.5 million.

Private finance participation

Only a few of the Region's MDPs assigned a specific role for private sector funding to help strengthen municipal management. Apart from the bond issue under **Tunisia I,** there is little evidence of a concerted effort by MDPs in the Region to stimulate private funding of municipal services at all. Even under that project, only minor private financing occurred at the municipal level, such as for detailed service design work for historic sites in Monastir. Significant private participation in municipal water authority in Sana'a has yet to occur as the **Republic of Yemen I** had hoped. Under **West Bank and Gaza II,** private financiers on whom the project design had initially relied to fund some municipal investments shied away as the conflict worsened in 2000.

Improved Service Provision

Investment priorities

Only two MDPs used estimates of ERRs to assess the priority of the project investments at appraisal and to measure the efficiency of project achievements at completion. Following careful analysis at completion, the **West Bank and Gaza III** yielded a very high ERR of 55 percent, exceeding even the appraisal estimate of 47 percent.

Project improvements to road and water infrastructure in 10 municipalities that accounted for 76 percent of all project costs generated very strong benefit streams, when compared with the dire without-project counterfactual. At completion, **Republic of Yemen I** yielded a 28 percent ERR (up from 25 percent at appraisal) that demonstrated the significant benefits obtained when municipal water supply shifts from high-cost tanker delivery to low-cost network provision. As well as demonstrating the positive results of the projects themselves, these examples demonstrate the feasibility of estimating ERRs even in the most challenging circumstances.

Procurement

There is little evidence of municipalities taking charge of procurement in a Region where this has largely remained a responsibility of central government authorities. Under **Republic of Yemen I,** delays were caused by the division of procurement responsibilities between the autonomous water authority for the municipality of Sana'a and the Ministry of Energy and Water. The ministry finally oversaw the international competitive bidding for the works, which led to cost savings at the outset, but these were offset by unfavorable foreign exchange rate movements.

Operations and maintenance

There were mixed results in this Region. Under **Tunisia I,** for example, the remote municipality of Kasserine (population 82,000) upgraded the Ezzouhour district of town and kept it in good condition through careful maintenance, sometimes involving local residents. But performance at the municipal level can vary under the same project. Thus, officials of the municipality of Ariana (population 237,395) saw the advantages of neglecting routine maintenance in upgraded areas. They felt that leaving drains blocked and pavement broken gave them a better chance of receiving central government aid to finance a complete replacement. The main shortcoming of the otherwise successful **Republic of Yemen I** was its inability to provide for adequate ongoing O&M of the facilities built under the project.

Services—Most affected sectors

Municipal infrastructure and services constituted the most numerous objectives in MDPs of the Region. The sectors for which MDPs sought strengthened municipal management in the Region included low-income neighborhood upgrading, urban street paving and drainage, water supply and basic sanitation, as well as other environmental improvements such as solid waste management.

MDPs achieved mixed results in upgrading and urban street and road improvements. **West Bank and Gaza I,** for instance, attended to planned rehabilitation work as well as subsequent damage caused by conflict. This would be done through 54 damage repair subprojects in 9 municipalities, sometimes exceeding targets, as in the case of 184 kilometers of roads built against a target of 100 kilometers. However, later border closures prevented the use of physical assets, which would deteriorate through lack of upkeep. **West Bank and Gaza III** successfully completed two road projects (13.2 kilometers) and rehabilitated 67 kilometers of roads. These improvements reduced travel costs and times by almost 50 percent in the project area.

West Bank and Gaza IV reached 61 municipalities through 2,200 subprojects in water and sanitation, roads, electricity, and solid waste, but the full extent to which this augmented services is not fully known. Under **Tunisia I,** the number of subprojects financed and their outlay exceeded expectations by 250 percent and 50 percent, respectively, but their impact on service levels was not fully documented. Improved streets gave people better access to their homes and businesses, as well as providing drainage and proper public lighting in central and residential areas of the client cities. A participatory approach adopted by many municipalities encouraged communities to contribute to the costs of some improvements, as IEG saw in Kasserine; there, 50 community leaders met with local officials to identify the priority investments for their own neighborhoods. This dialogue appears to have developed greater understanding of the need for cost recovery. Twice as much in direct taxation was collected in Kasserine after the project as before.

Republic of Yemen I helped improve the living conditions in the Akama neighborhood of Sana'a by reducing raw sewage flooding in residential areas, thanks to 7,500 additional households being connected to the sewerage system, seven times the original target. Water supply also increased, though not as much as targeted, because only 5,000 households of the targeted 18,500 were connected. However, despite replacing 21,500 water meters and rehabilitating 30 kilometers of pipelines, the project did not succeed in reducing unaccounted-for water.

West Bank and Gaza II constructed or rehabilitated 64 kilometers of water lines (as well as 77 kilometers of roads, which was several times the original targets), but it is not clear if this was due to any dilution in design criteria. **West Bank and Gaza III** expanded the water network in several small settlements that reported 90 percent of their population receiving a 24-hour piped water supply. The extent of this achievement cannot be fully evaluated, however, for lack of baseline data about the level of before-project service, or even data on the population served.

Services—Private provision

MDPs in the Region did not put much emphasis on increasing the private provision of municipal services, and there was little progress where such attempts were made. Under **Republic of Yemen I,** the intended private management of the Sana'a water agency had yet to be implemented and the government remained uncommitted. Under **West Bank and Gaza II,** renewed conflict in 2000 precluded any increase in private sector participation.

The otherwise very successful **Tunisia I** made little progress in improving the incentive framework for building partnerships with the private sector and municipalities. Under **Morocco's MDP,** both the government's commitments for the rehabilitation process and

---

Box F.1: Key to MDPs Referred to in Text

Arab Republic of Egypt: Alexandria Development. **Islamic Republic of Iran:** Urban Upgrading & Housing Reform. **Jordan:** I—Regional & Local Development; II—Cultural Heritage, Tourism & Urban Development. **Lebanon:** I—First Municipal Infrastructure; II—Cultural Heritage & Urban Development. **Morocco:** Fes Medina Rehabilitation. **Tunisia:** I—Municipal Sector Investment; II—Second Municipal Development; III—Transport Sector Investment; IV—Third Municipal Development. **West Bank and Gaza:** I—Municipal Development; II—Bethlehem 2000; III—Second Municipal Infrastructure Development; IV—Emergency Municipal Services Rehabilitation. **Republic of Yemen:** I—Sana'a Water Supply & Sanitation; II—Taiz Municipal Development & Flood Protection; III—Port Cities Development Program.

Source: IEG.

---

projections for leveraging private sector investments fell far short of expectations during the project period, and it appears too early to assess whether projections made at project closing will be realized to any significant extent.

Income level of beneficiaries—Poverty reduction

There was no explicit focus on the income levels of beneficiaries or on poverty reduction in most MDPs in the Region. Even in the few cases where this was directly or indirectly attempted, the results fell short of targets. **West Bank and Gaza IV** managed to create 270,000 person-days of employment for unskilled workers, but this was short of the target of 400,000, after some of the resources allocated to employment generation were transferred to service provision instead.

Under **Morocco's MDP,** only 20 percent of the beneficiaries were classified as poor. Under **Tunisia I,** there was no clear focus on poverty reduction. Several stakeholders, especially in the municipalities themselves, appeared to be unfamiliar with the Bank's mission relating to poverty reduction and saw no contradiction in project investment being made in higher-income areas.

Conclusions

- Development programs in the Region can make more use of municipalities as partners in service provision, even where central governments prefer to retain overall responsibility themselves.
- Robust evidence from the Region shows that MDPs can improve the performance of municipal finance, and the potential for strengthening this dimension of municipal management appears to be under-exploited.
- Frequent claims that M&E and ERR exercises are too complex and costly to implement in volatile country conditions are not borne out by experience in this Region, where a few experiences have been quite successful.

APPENDIX G: BANKING ON MUNICIPALITIES: WORLD BANK SUPPORT IN SOUTH ASIA

Bank Support

Although South Asia is one of the world's less urbanized regions, more than 431 million people, 29 percent of the total population, live in the Region's cities. Through just 12 MDPs active during the past decade (1998–2008), the World Bank committed $1.3 billion. This small portfolio aimed to strengthen the management of 146 municipalities in 6 countries. By number of MDPs, the most active borrowers were India (4 projects); Pakistan (3); and Bangladesh (2); Afghanistan, Bhutan, and Sri Lanka hosted 1 each. Thus, all but two of the Region's MDPs were in low-income countries. With an urban population of 4.5 million—16 percent of the total—Nepal was the only large country in the Region not to host an MDP.

Portfolio Performance

Only three of the seven completed MDPs in this Region (43 percent) achieved a satisfactory outcome, making this the weakest of the Bank's Regional MDP portfolios. Only four of them had satisfactory ratings for both Bank and borrower performance.

The only fully satisfactory completed operation in the portfolio was **India II,** which set up a municipal development fund that financed investments by municipalities in the southern state of Tamil Nadu. This operation built on more than 20 years of continuous Bank assistance to the urban development of Tamil Nadu and its capital Chennai. By introducing computerized accounting and modern financial management methods, **India II** helped 45 municipalities in the state prepare "corporative development plans" to help determine their priority investments. This support also helped Tamil Nadu's

Table G.1: Summary of MDP Portfolio, 1998–2008	
Completed (number)	7
Completed MDPs (% satisfactory)	43
Ongoing MDPs (number)	5
IBRD Commitments (US$ million)	671
IDA Commitments (US$ million)	673
Commitments per completed MDP (US$ million)	88
Commitments per ongoing MDP (US$ million)	146
Wholesale MDPs (number)	4
Retail MDPs (number)	8
Countries served (number)	6
Municipalities served (number)	146

Source: World Bank data.

Note: IBRD = International Bank for Reconstruction and Development; IDA = International Development Association; MDP = municipal development project.

second-largest city Madurai (population 909,908) successfully issue municipal bonds for the first time, to finance an inner ring road.

Several MDPs performed poorly. Implementation of **Bangladesh I** was hostage to land-acquisition problems and a lack of coordination between borrower agencies, resulting in resettlement not complying with Bank guidelines. In addition, municipal financial management remained weak. **Sri Lanka's MDP** suffered from poor design that did not take into account the public opposition to the project's plans for solid waste disposal. The design was also based on an incomplete understanding of the baseline water quality of the polluted Beira Lake in the capital Colombo (population 2.3 million) that the project aimed to improve. The municipal management in Colombo barely changed as a result of the project.

Figure G.1: MDP Portfolio Performance, Fiscal 1998–2008

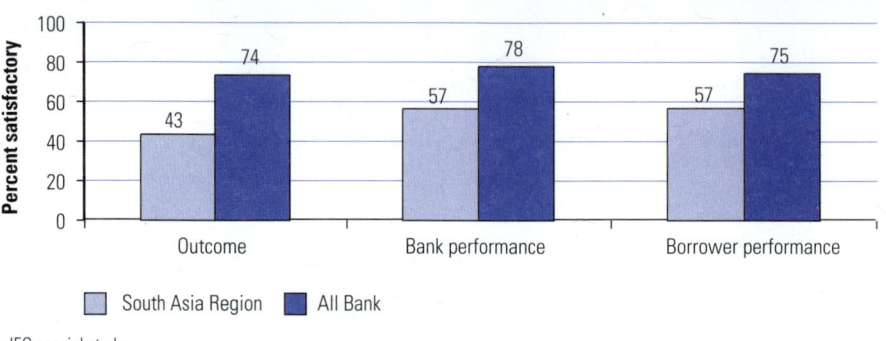

Source: IEG special study.
Note: MDP = municipal development project.

Pakistan II did not succeed in the Northwest Frontier largely because efficiency criteria for selecting subprojects and financing them were outweighed by political factors that determined the choices made. **Bhutan's MDP** did not succeed primarily because the design overestimated the management capabilities of local municipalities.

Better City Planning

More information

India II provided technical assistance to 50 municipalities, called urban local bodies in Tamil Nadu. As a result, 46 local municipalities have prepared city corporate plans with a mapping of urban infrastructure using important baseline data. However, these plans have yet to become key drivers of local municipal development, even though they have facilitated municipal access to loans by the Tamil Nadu Urban Development Fund, itself established by an earlier MDP project. The need for systematic data collection is now better appreciated; in fact, the State Municipal Administration and Water Supply Department plans to assist local municipalities prepare a human development index for such basic services as water supply, sanitation, health, poverty alleviation, and access to basic needs.

Under the **Sri Lanka MDP,** the Colombo master plan benefited from the project's provision of a geographic information system for the Urban Development Authority, but little expertise was passed on to the Colombo municipality that is responsible for cadastral and land-use applications for the geographic information system.

Monitoring and evaluation

M&E was weak in MDPs. Its weakness came from too much focus on the delivery of project outputs and too little on project impacts gained through achieving the MDP objectives. This M&E shortcoming was even evident in the otherwise well-performing **India II,** which gave little attention to measuring the achievement of municipal service improvements, let alone the

Table G.2: Municipal Management Focus of Region's Portfolio

Share of all MDPs with a project design focus on:	Completed	Ongoing
City planning		
In objectives (%)	29	0
In components (%)	0	67
Municipal finance		
In objectives (%)	57	60
In components (%)	43	60
Service delivery		
In objectives (%)	100	100
In components (%)	100	100
Number of all MDPs	7	5

Source: IEG special study.
Note: MDP = municipal development project.

impact on beneficiaries. For instance, a completed bus stand was treated as fully achieved, even though it had not started functioning because it did not have the necessary official permits. Even targets that had measurable goals did not have baseline data to compare against.

However, some evaluation studies carried out at the end of **India II** to inform the follow-up project did provide useful information on urban environmental indicators. Some of the larger municipalities collect regular and reliable information on service status and achievements, such as water supply per capita per day, though this is still not typical of most municipalities in the state. In **Pakistan II,** too, the M&E system was overly focused on inputs and outputs, and even data that were collected were not used to improve implementation.

Under the **Sri Lanka MDP,** the lack of baseline data on the original condition of the Beira Lake water and the absence of systematic monitoring of changes to it made it impossible to assess properly the results obtained through the project.

Urban and spatial planning
Apart from the update to the Colombo master plan under the **Sri Lanka MDP,** there was not much evidence of MDP impact on this in the Region.

Investment planning and strategies
India II in Tamil Nadu provided consultant technical assistance to and facilitated exchanges among 45 municipalities to help each prepare corporate plans that set out their investment priorities for the following 10 years.

Stronger Municipal Finances

Better financial management
Significant efforts to improve financial management were mainly confined to India and Bhutan, with positive results in India but less so in Bhutan. **India I** and **II** helped strengthen local municipal capacity in finance and accounting, including computerization. This occurred through training (35 freestanding courses) for finance and account-

ing officials, as well as for elected representatives. This training helped most local municipalities adopt the accrual accounting system and computerize the collection of municipal taxes and fees. Now the collection performance of several local municipalities can be monitored in real time, making information quickly accessible for decision makers at the municipal and state level. Compliance has become easier to monitor, and users find it easier to pay their taxes.

Under the **Bhutan MDP,** financial reporting during implementation was weak and was made worse by lack of technical support within the country for the computerized financial management system that had been customized for the project. On a related matter, much needs to be done to build financial systems for cost recovery.

Mobilizing own revenues
Under **India I,** Tiruchirapalli municipality (population 775,484) reported an increase of 60 percent in revenue between fiscal 2004 and 2005. The municipality used the additional revenue to undertake new infrastructure investments of its own, such as the water supply in the Srirangam area. The Madurai municipality increased property tax collections by 20 percent during fiscal 2004–05, compared to 6 percent for the previous year. In terms of direct cost recovery from MDP investment, there is little evidence of significant results in the Region.

Under **India I,** little was done to simplify procedures for revising bus fares or to strengthen the transport corporation in Chennai (population 4.3 million), which continued to be a loss-making entity, unable to invest in or expand services. Under **Bangladesh I,** the cost-recovery component through Agrani Bank loans was cancelled, and the property tax collection system remained unchanged.

Municipal creditworthiness and debt management
India II encouraged municipalities in Tamil Nadu to become creditworthy to have better access to loans awarded by the Tamil Nadu Urban Development Fund (TNUDF). Under this arrangement,

local municipalities were given easy access to discuss and access the TNUDF's knowledge base of innovative funding, for which there was a high demand. By March 2005, 39 percent of TNUDF's portfolio related to investments in bridges and roads, 38 percent to sewerage and sanitation, and 17 percent to water supply.

The state's second largest city, Madurai (population 909,908), went one step further. With technical assistance provided through the project, the municipality issued bonds to raise funds to pay for the construction of an inner ring road that today yields $1.4 million per annum in toll charges.

Private finance participation

MDPs in this Region did little to achieve private financing of projects. **India I** and **II** came closest by encouraging the TNUDF to create near-market conditions for municipal investment that would begin to interest private financiers. But **India I** failed to promote the intended private participation of shelter and land development in the slums of Chennai because of the lack of interest on the part of private developers.

Improved Service Provision

Investment priorities

Estimates for ERRs were rarely made for MDPs in the Region. One exception was **Bhutan's MDP,** which yielded a 25.8 percent ERR at completion, according to government estimates.

Procurement

As in other Regions, MDPs involved local municipalities more in preparing and sometimes fully managing procurement. Although some shortcomings were still reported, the procurement experience of **Pakistan I** highlighted the effectiveness of spot checks, especially in the municipality of Lahore (population 6.3 million), on the good faith of bids. Such checks helped prevent insider trading and the formation of local cartels.

Under the **Sri Lanka MDP,** both the municipality of Colombo and the national authorities perfected their skills in prequalifying bidders, so that tenders always included high-quality techni-

cal solutions. The **Bhutan MDP** introduced competitive procurement for municipal works for the first time in that country, even though municipal capacity in this area remains weak.

Operations and maintenance

MDPs in the Region rarely addressed municipal responsibilities for O&M, and this neglect remains an ongoing concern. Thus, the benefits from physical works under **Bangladesh I,** for instance, are unlikely to be sustained because of continued neglect of maintenance. Despite progress in improving sewerage under **Pakistan I,** there too municipalities' O&M is adequate. As result, the uncollected waste accumulating in sewers and drains undermines the benefits of the upgrading that was done.

Services—Most affected sectors

MDPs in India, Bhutan, Bangladesh, Pakistan, and Sri Lanka helped improve urban services and related infrastructure. In Tamil Nadu, **India I** and **II** contributed positively to services, infrastructure, and security in slums and made some improvements to urban roads and transport services. The projects improved living conditions in 489 slums (against a target of 590), housing 76,000 people—or 5 percent of the slum population—in the 10 largest agglomerations in the state. This was done by providing paved pathways, drains, streetlights, public fountains and baths, and tenure security. Beneficiaries reported health improvements and greater social acceptance. There were some shortfalls in transport services: only 4 of 10 depots and 7 of 10 terminals were completed. The widening of the inner ring road in Chennai was only partially completed because of difficulties in acquiring necessary land. For the transport corporation in Chennai, 1,595 bus chassis were procured, but they could not all be used because of financial constraints.

Under **Pakistan I,** about 300,000 low-income people in Lahore, Gujranwala, Sialkot, and Multan benefited from slum upgrading. In Lahore, 21 major roads were improved and new street lighting and traffic signals were installed. But the construction of stabilization ponds for sewage treatment in Lahore was deferred for a later project. **Pakistan II's** upgrading reportedly reached 90 communities with 550,000 beneficiaries and engaged in road construction that saved travel time and improved environmental conditions, but evidence for these assertions was not always clear. They must be in doubt, given the reports of lack of coordination among stakeholders and of failed project infrastructure that had to be rebuilt prematurely.

Following **Bangladesh I,** 90 percent of slum dwellers in three Dhaka slums (Islambagh, Raulpur, and Shaheednagar) reported improved living conditions through construction of 482 latrines. But the project faced implementation shortfalls, again because of difficulties in acquiring land. The **Bhutan MDP** helped improve the quality of life in 10 towns through enhancements to water supply and other urban infrastructure, although the results were short of targets. The project experience enabled municipalities there to participate in the environmental screening of subprojects. Under the **Bhutan MDP,** there was improved interaction between central and local governments on the environmental screening of urban investments. A beneficiary survey revealed that 73–83 percent of respondents in 3 towns considered the water supply to have improved, but this result has to be set against surveys in towns that were not covered by the project that also reported similar improvements.

The **Sri Lanka MDP** did not improve solid waste management in Colombo, despite the city building a large-scale compost operation, which the Bank had initially suggested was not the best technical solution to the problem. The project had greater success in reducing wastewater pollution in the Beira Lake catchment area. An industrial waste system was completed under the project, and several lakeside dwellings were hooked up to the sewerage system.

Income levels of beneficiaries—Poverty reduction

There is evidence that the modest results of the Region's MDP portfolio did nevertheless bring some benefits to the poor. **Pakistan II** aimed to reach low-income groups in the Northwest

---

> ### Box G.1: Key to MDPs Referred to in Text
>
> **Afghanistan:** Kabul Urban Reconstruction. **Bangladesh:** I—Urban Development; II—Municipal Services. **Bhutan:** Urban Development. **India:** I—Tamil Nadu Urban Development; II—Tamil Nadu Second Urban Development; III—Karnataka Municipal Reform; IV—Third Tamil Nadu Urban Development. **Pakistan:** I—Punjab Urban Development; II—Northwest Frontier Province Community Infrastructure; III—Punjab Municipal Services Improvement. **Sri Lanka:** Colombo Environment Improvement.
>
> *Source:* IEG.

Frontier Province, but the effectiveness of poverty targeting was unclear because of political interference in beneficiary identification. Improvements in living conditions cannot be attributed to the project.

Under **India I,** a cross-subsidy from the sale of a small number of lots for middle- and higher-income households helped finance a number of serviced plots for the poorest households, which included common open spaces that made best use of the land available. Under **India II,** benefits reached the poor through slum upgrading in particular. Also an integrated sanitation program provided public complexes with toilets and washing areas in underserved areas such as slums. Beneficiaries—who are typically poor—reported a substantial improvement in their quality of life. As a result, open defecation was reported to have decreased by 80 percent.

Conclusions

- The positive experiences of **India I** and **II,** involving almost 20 years of continuous Bank assistance to urban development in the state of Tamil Nadu, suggest that adapting a wholesale, step-by-step approach to a particular context over a sustained period can yield positive results.
- **India II** has contributed to improving urban infrastructure services in Tamil Nadu, directly through projects funded by TNUDF and indirectly through capacity building in municipalities that have made additional infrastructure investments using their own funds.

- Even in projects that otherwise perform weakly, municipal management can be strengthened by increasing the responsibilities of local government for procurement of works and goods, as experience in Bhutan and Sri Lanka showed. To minimize risks, spot checks can be necessary, such as those made in **Pakistan I.**

Principles

As a meta-evaluation, this assessment was designed to assemble and review existing IEG evaluation findings about Bank support for MDPs from Project Performance Assessment Reports (PPARs) and IEG Reviews of Implementation Completion Reports (ICR Reviews). As such, it is analogous to a literature review, where the literature in this case consists of previous IEG assessments, particularly in PPARs.

The 1998–2008 period of the review, chosen for its immediate relevance to ongoing work in this area, encompasses a portfolio of all MDPs completed since 1998, as well as those still ongoing. MDPs that *exited* between 1998 and 2008 generally have an ICR, a self-evaluation prepared by the Bank's Operations Region, and an ICR Review, an independent assessment done by IEG based on the ICR. About one-third of the *closed* MDPs were approved within the same decade; the approvals of the remaining two-thirds in some cases dated as far back as 1988. This study considered all MDPs that were completed since 1998 and those that are still ongoing.

Municipalities and Cities

The study used the online World Gazetteer database in Germany, which contains details of more than 167,000 named municipalities. Records include census populations, geographic coordinates of location, and the type of local authority, in English and in the local language. In extracting municipality-level population figures from this database, IEG found that 31,000 larger municipalities, each having 12,500 or more inhabitants, were home to 3.25 billion people, approximately half the world's population, and

very close to the 50 percent now reported to live in urban areas.

The correspondence is not exact, however, for three reasons. First, a larger urban municipality with an extensive jurisdiction might contain some rural inhabitants on its periphery, especially if the jurisdiction is large. Second, because concepts of urban population vary from country to country, a local definition of "urban" may not always be comparable with the criterion used in this study. Third, it will not be the case of a single metropolitan area composed of multiple municipal jurisdictions—in such cases, there would be one city, yet many municipalities. IEG's methodology may overstate the number of cities, because it counts peripheral rural populations in larger municipalities as urban. To ensure that estimates of the number of cities are reliable, IEG triangulated the results with estimates of the urban population from the World Development Indicators. The calibration at the country level confirmed IEG estimates for this study to be within ±10 percent of the World Development Indicators estimates.

The MDP Portfolio

The study portfolio of MDP operations was identified through an internal Bank database. As a first cut, IEG identified 231 operations classified by one of the Bank's four related activity codes: #71 Municipal Management, #72 Municipal Finance, #73 Municipal Services, and #74 Subnational Government Administration. Then IEG conducted a keyword search for projects without these codes, but with the words *municipal* (and variants), *city/cities, local government,* and *local authorities* to identify projects that worked closely with municipalities and cities, but not classified as such by one of the Bank's activity codes.

Next the study team eliminated 68 of these operations after finding that they did not have municipal management objectives or components despite the activity coding. That left 163 MDP projects.

IEG sent the preliminary listings (by Region) of this portfolio to Bank urban staff in each Operational Region, requesting that they help identify any Type I and Type II errors in the lists by pointing out operations that had been included that were not MDPs, and other operations that were MDPs but were not in the lists. Thanks to excellent responses, IEG was able to exclude some projects that did not fully meet the criterion of a direct focus on improving municipal management. IEG could also include additional projects overlooked in its first search, ones that lacked a municipal activity code but that were focused on strengthening municipal management. As a result of this dialogue with the Regions, 14 projects were dropped from the portfolio and 41 projects were added, resulting in a portfolio of 190 MDPs.

The final study portfolio of 190 MDPs included 114 *closed* MDPs and 76 *ongoing* MDPs. IEG project reviews are only available for *closed* MDPs, of course. *Entry* MDPs have not yet been evaluated by IEG, nor will they be through this study. But they are considered in the present study, where they stand as evidence of the lessons of evaluated *closed* MDPs being carried forward.

About 92 percent of the MDPs in the portfolio are mapped to the Sustainable Development Network. Sixty-six percent are mapped to the Urban Sector Board, with 12 percent to the Water Sector Board, 9 percent to the Transport Sector Board, and 5 percent to the Environment Sector Board.

IEG Evaluations

During fiscal 1998–2008, IEG completed 17 PPARs—all in different countries, covering 24 MDPs, about one-fifth of completed MDPs. The MDPs chosen for the PPARs were not randomly selected. When choosing them, IEG applied various considerations: providing input for IEG thematic studies and Country Assistance Evaluations as well as ensuring that all six Bank operating Regions were covered.

Criteria for selection of the 24 MDPs chosen for IEG field review through PPARs were varied. As far as this study itself is concerned, the most relevant criterion was to use the PPAR as an input. This applied to **The Gambia MDP, Tanzania I, Indonesia II, VI,** and **IX, Russia IV,** and **India I** and **II.** Others were chosen to feed into IEG Country Assistance Evaluations, including **Georgia I, II,** and **III** and **Colombia I** and **IV.** Some were selected from countries where IEG evaluations of urban projects had been thin, namely **China III, IV,** and **VII, Sri Lanka,** and **Uzbekistan.** The remaining projects were part of IEG's regular program of PPAR assessments.

Prior to this study and as per normal practice, IEG carried out 114 desk ICR reviews, covering 100 percent of the completed MDPs. From the ICR Reviews, information on the objectives, components, and lessons of each operation were compiled into the study database.

Municipal Management Themes

To identify whether an MDP supported one of the study's three municipal management themes, IEG conducted keyword searches of the objectives formulated for each operation. When the appropriate keyword was found, the MDP was classified as being focused on the particular theme in question. For each theme, the following key words (in parentheses) were used: (i) *city planning* (plan*, strateg*, program*, *tech*, *inst*, *train*, *capa*, *manag*); (ii) *municipal finances* (finance*, fund*, budget*, fin*/manag*); and (iii) *service provision* (service, infras*, water, env*). Because the three are not mutually exclusive categories, it was possible for an individual MDP to focus on more than one theme at the same time.

IEG adopted a similar procedure to identify the relevance of the design of an MDP, through similar keyword searches of the description of a project's components. As with the focus on objectives, an MDP's design could cover more than just one of the study's themes.

Levels of Assessment of MDP Portfolio

The most intensive assessment in this study, presented in the main report, was based on earlier evaluation findings of the 24 MDPs reviewed by PPARs. The study also looked more broadly, reporting the findings in the Regional annexes to this report, at evaluation findings of all 114 completed MDPs for which there are ICR Reviews. Finally, the study also considered, without evaluation, the 76 ongoing MDPs, in order to review how the current portfolio continues to address the issues raised by this evaluation. Among other things, the different sets of MDPs explain the discontinuous nomenclature of individual MDPs in the main report and the extra countries and MDPs referred to in the annexes.

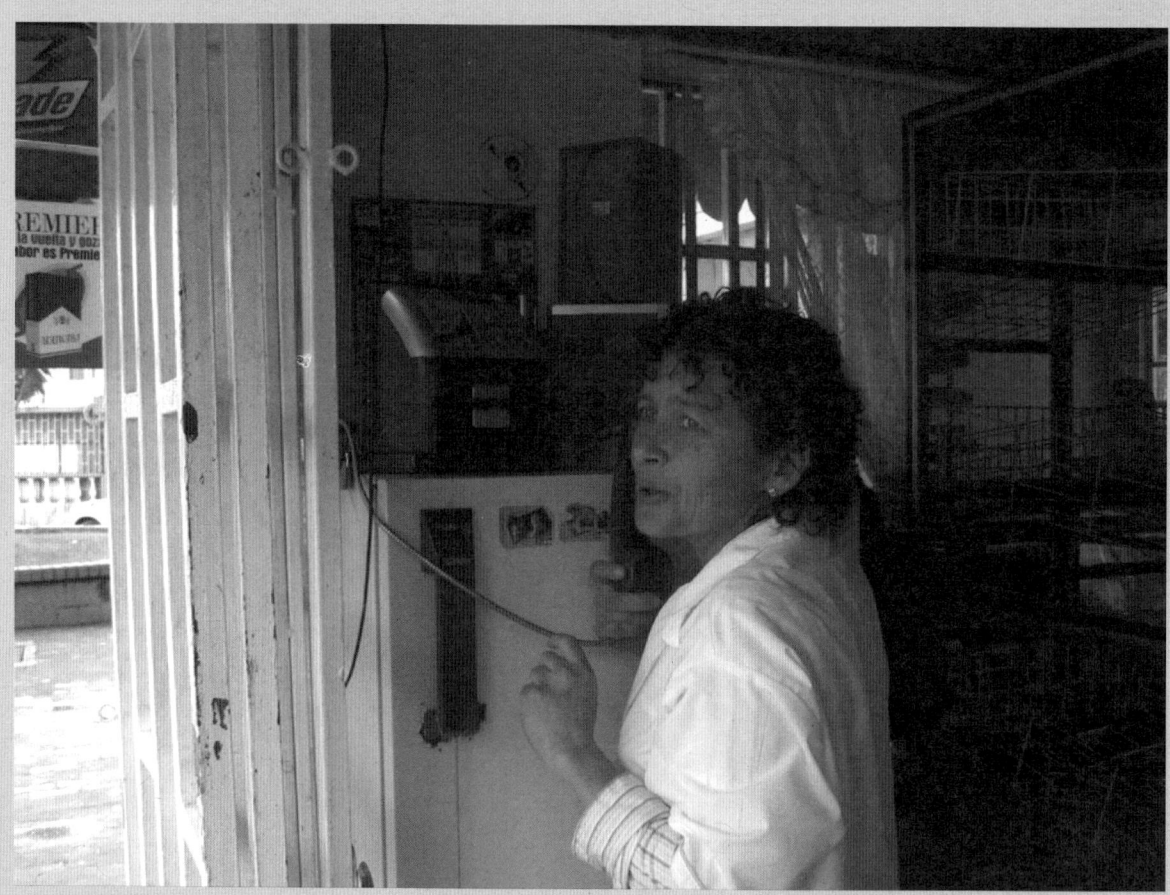

Using new municipal services in Pereira, Colombia. Photo courtesy of Roy Gilbert.

Management Comments

1. IEG confirms that its assessment is based on how often MDPs refer explicitly to the poor or poverty reduction in their objectives. MDPs with poverty reduction components or actions that lack a supporting objective would not be counted. Explicit poverty reduction objectives would increase the count of MDPs covering poverty. They would also make the aims and purpose of their poverty-related actions clear.

Chapter 1

1. Launched in 2006 and reporting in 2008, the Commission had 22 leading practitioners, mostly from the developing world. They were charged with drafting the policy implications for sustained economic growth. The Commission was sponsored by bilateral and multilateral donors (including the World Bank).

2. In some countries, municipalities might go by other designations not used in this report. Commune, county, *opstina,* and *wilayat* are just a few examples. Whatever term is used, the generic municipality is typically headed by an elected or designated council and mayor, who appoint technical staff and officials to carry out day-to-day municipal management. Also, as used in this report, the term *city* refers to a built-up spatial concentration of wealth, population, and economic activity, as in the 2009 WDR *Reshaping Economic Geography* (World Bank 2008).

3. Currently, the largest municipality in the world is Chongqing, China, with an estimated population of 31.6 million people.

4. Figures are taken from www.world-gazetteer.com in Germany.

5. The study does not cover two exceptional arrangements. The first is where several contiguous municipalities manage a single megacity, often constituting a metropolitan area; this example did not arise in the Bank portfolio reviewed here. The second arrangement is where a single municipality manages several very

small settlements, but this usually occurs in lightly populated rural areas, which are not covered by the present study.

6. This portfolio was identified in three stages. First, a keyword search identified all operations within the 1998–2008 period whose formal Bank coded activity included the word "municipal" or "subnational." This gave a preliminary total of 231 projects. Second, 68 of these operations were eliminated when closer review revealed that, despite their activity coding, they did not have municipal management objectives or components. This lowered the count to 163 projects. For the third stage, IEG sent the list of 163 to all Bank urban sector staff, inviting them to comment and make corrections. Feedback from these staff led to the removal of 14 and the addition of 41 projects. These adjustments resulted in a portfolio of 190 MDPs (details in appendix H).

7. To directly assess the effectiveness of municipal management support, 17 of these 24 PPAR MDPs were purposefully selected from all Regions to serve as building blocks for the present study. The remaining 7 were chosen for other reasons, including ensuring IEG coverage of under-evaluated countries and more detailed evaluations of operations whose rating by IEG differed from the Region's.

Chapter 2

1. Project documentation and government reports may inform the number of municipalities served, but without identifying each one by name, especially when a large number of municipalities is involved. Evaluation would have been easier if all Implementation Completion Reports for MDPs routinely reported the name, population, and project investment in each municipality supported. In using these sources to estimate the total number of municipalities and cities served for this study, IEG exercised care to avoid double counting municipalities that may have been assisted by more than one MDP operation in a particular country. Finding out just

how many cities were assisted, something that has not been clearly done previously by the Bank, was one of the questions driving this evaluation.

2. IEG uses 20,000 municipalities as the denominator here. Countries hosting Bank-financed MDPs account for the vast majority of all developing country municipalities—some 18,000, or 90 percent of the total.

3. Examples of apex agencies in wholesale MDPs reviewed by PPARs include Georgia II and III—The Municipal Fund of Georgia, www.mdf.org.ge/; Brazil II—Ceará state government, Secretariat of Cities, http://www.cidades.ce .gov.br/; Chile II—Subsecretariat of Regional Development, http://www.subdere.gov.cl; Colombia I and IV—Local Development Fund (FINDETER), http://www.findeter.gov.co/.

4. An extreme case of this is the municipality of Chongquing, whose 82,000 square kilometer jurisdiction embraces more than 30 million people in 7 large and 25 small and medium-sized cities, as well as numerous tiny rural settlements. This extensive area is more than 10 times the 8,051 square kilometers of the municipality of Sao Paulo, Brazil, which is home to 10.4 million people.

5. For this, the study transformed the six category outcome ratings into a six-point numerical scale, where highly satisfactory = 6, satisfactory = 5, and so on. The difference of the mean scores proved to be highly significant (t statistic = 2.3012, significant at 99 percent). On this scale, the mean of the wholesale MDP rating was 4.46 (satisfactory), and the mean of the retail MDP outcome was 3.97 (moderately satisfactory).

6. This difference of means was found to be statistically significant (t statistic = 2.5821, significant at 99 percent).

7. This compares unfavorably with an earlier IEG finding for the urban portfolio as a whole, which was 53 percent of completed projects with poverty-focused objectives; 69 percent of ongoing projects had this focus (IEG 2004, pp. 11–12).

Chapter 3

1. This report provides ratings of 11 specific MDP achievements across the municipal management dimensions of planning, finance, and service provision. For the municipal information system results in this instance and for all others, the assessments are based on the observed efficacy of the actual results obtained by the specific management improvement. A rating of "substantial" means that the expected result was fully achieved; a rating of "modest" means that the expected result was only partly achieved.

2. Since IEG began rating M&E performance in July 2007, only 18 percent of all completed MDPs achieved a rating of substantial for their M&E.

3. This is now known more generically as a Development Policy Loan.

4. For more detailed evaluation findings on the Cities Alliance, see IEG (2008).

Chapter 4

1. Taking own revenues and transfers together, total municipal revenues can account for up to 6 percent of gross domestic product (Shah 2006, p. 35).

2. An earlier IEG evaluation of MDPs in Brazil (IEG 1999) found that these operations obtained robust financial results; the financial performance of municipalities receiving MDP support was significantly stronger than that of unassisted municipalities.

3. A primary objective of the World Bank Group's new subnational finance facility is to strengthen a (municipal) borrower's ability to deliver key infrastructure services and to improve their efficiency and accountability as services providers: http://www.ifc.org/ifcext/ subnationalfinance.nsf/ Content/Home.

Annez, Patricia, Gwenaelle Huet, and George Peterson. 2008. *Lessons for the Urban Century: Decentralized Infrastructure Funds in the World Bank*. Directions for Development Series—Infrastructure. Washington, DC: World Bank.

Boadway, Robin, and Anwar Shah (eds.). 2007. *Intergovernmental Fiscal Transfers*. Washington DC: World Bank.

Spence, Michael. 2008. "The Growth Report: Strategies for Sustained Growth and Inclusive Development." Commission on Growth and Development Final Report, Washington, DC.

Davis, Mike. 2006. *Planet of Slums*. London, Verso.

Duranton, Gilles. 2008. "Cities: Engines of Growth and Prosperity for Developing Countries?" Working Paper No. 12 of Commission on Growth and Development, World Bank, Washington DC.

IEG (Independent Evaluation Group). 2008. "The Cities Alliance." *Global Program Review* Vol. 1 (4).

———. 2004. *Improving the Lives of the Poor through Investment in Cities: An Update on the Performance of the World Bank's Urban Portfolio*. Washington, DC: World Bank.

———. 1999. *Developing Towns and Cities: Lessons from Brazil and the Philippines*. Washington, DC: World Bank.

Leautier, Frannie. 2006. *Cities in a Globalizing World: Governance, Performance and Sustainability*. Washington DC, World Bank Institute.

Peterson, George E., and Patricia Clarke Annez. 2007. *Financing Cities: Fiscal Responsibility and Urban Infrastructure in Brazil, China, India, Poland and South Africa*. Los Angeles: Sage Publications.

Ravallion, Martin, Shaohua Chen, and Prem Sangraula. 2007. "New Evidence on the Urbanization of Global Poverty." Policy Research Paper 4199, World Bank, Washington, DC.

Shah, Anwar (ed.). 2006. *Local Governance in Developing Countries*. Washington, DC: World Bank.

UNFPA (United Nations Population Fund). 2007. *State of the World Population 2007: Unleashing the Potential of Urban Growth*. New York: UNFPA.

World Bank. 2008. *World Development Report 2009: Reshaping Economic Geography*. Washington, DC, and New York: World Bank and Oxford University Press.

———. 2006. "China: Governance, Investment Climate, and Harmonious Society: Competitiveness Enhancements for 120 Cities in China." Poverty Reduction and Economic Management, Financial and Private Sector Development Unit, East Asia and Pacific Region Report No. 37759-CN, World Bank, Washington DC.

———. 2004. *World Development Report 2004: Making Services Work for Poor People*. Washington, DC, and New York: World Bank and Oxford University Press.

———. 2003. *World Development Report 2003: Sustainable Development in a Dynamic World—Transforming Institutions, Growth, and Quality of Life*. Washington, DC, and New York: World Bank and Oxford University Press.

———. 2002. *World Development Report 2002: Building Institutions for Markets*. Washington, DC, and New York: World Bank and Oxford University Press.

———. 2001. *World Development Report 2001: Attacking Poverty*. Washington, DC, and New York: World Bank and Oxford University Press.

———. 2000a. *Cities in Transition: World Bank Urban and Local Government Strategy*. Washington, DC: World Bank.

———. 2000b. *World Development Report 1999/2000: Entering the 21st Century*. Washington, DC, and New York: World Bank and Oxford University Press.

———. 1989. "Report of the Task Force on Financial Sector Operations." Report No. R89-163, World Bank, Washington, DC.

Yussuf, Shahid. 2007. "About Urban Mega Regions: Knowns and Unknowns." Policy Research Paper 4252, World Bank, Washington, DC.